FEMALE INDIGENOUS HEROES

FEMALE INDIGENOUS HEROES

51 NORTH AMERICAN WOMEN FROM THE 1800S TO TODAY

Artists, Activists, Athletes, and More

KATRINA M. PHILLIPS

ILLUSTRATIONS BY TΔI

Callisto Kids,
An imprint of Callisto Publishing LLC

Published by Callisto Publishing LLC C/O Sourcebooks LLC
P.O. Box 4410, Naperville, Illinois 60567-4410
(630) 961-3900
callistopublishing.com

Text by Katrina Phillips
Illustrations by TΔI

Series Designer: Brian Lewis
Art Director: Angela Navarra
Art Producer: Stacey Stambaugh
Editor: Kristen Depken
Production Editor: Rachel Taenzler
Production Designer: Martin Worthington

Source of Production: 1010 Printing Asia Limited, Kwun Tong, Hong Kong, China
Date of Production: January 2026
Run Number: 5052136

Printed and bound in China.
OGP 10 9 8 7 6 5 4 3 2 1

For Leo and Max

CONTENTS

INTRODUCTION

What does it mean to be a hero? A hero motivates others and works to make the world a better place. A hero makes a difference, whether they're saving lives or bringing people together. A hero is brave, whether they're standing up for what's right or calling for change.

This book highlights **Native** and **Indigenous** women from different backgrounds, different life experiences, and different eras who all have one thing in common: they're some of the countless Native and Indigenous women throughout history whose actions, words, or discoveries have served as an inspiration to others.

The women in this book are artists, athletes, and activists. They're in medicine, the military, and the media. Many of them have been called "the first"—the first Native woman to lead their nation, the first Native prima ballerina, or the first Native woman to go to space. Some may be famous, and others have stories that might be new to you.

This book is for everyone. We all need heroes in our lives, and we all need people we can look up to. I hope this book inspires *you* to make a difference in your own way.

JANE JOHNSTON SCHOOLCRAFT

(1800–1842)

Jane Johnston Schoolcraft was an Ojibwe poet and writer. She's also considered the first known Native woman writer.

Jane was born in Sault Ste. Marie (in what's now the state of Michigan) in 1800. Her mother, Ozhaguscodaywayquay [Oh-zhah-gus-co-day-way-kway], was Ojibwe, and she came from a long line of respected leaders. Jane's father, John Johnston, was a Scots-Irish fur trader. Jane was also known by her Ojibwe name, Bamewawagezhikaquay [Bah-may-wah-wah -gay-zhihk-ah-kway]. Her name translates to "Woman of the Sound the Stars Make Rushing Through the Sky."

Jane and her seven brothers and sisters grew up speaking both Ojibwe and English. Their mother taught them Ojibwe stories, and she taught them about Ojibwe history and culture. Their father loved to read. Jane started writing poetry when she was about 15. She never published her poems, but she wrote around 50 poems in both English and Ojibwe. She wrote poems about things found in nature, and she wrote poems about loneliness and grieving. Her poems often reflected her feelings.

With her father and one of her brothers, she also wrote down Ojibwe songs and stories and translated them into English.

In 1822, American officials sent a man named Henry Rowe Schoolcraft to the Great Lakes. Schoolcraft was told to collect information about Ojibwe people and their language. Jane became his main source, and they later married.

Henry and Jane moved to New York City in 1841, and Jane died in 1842. While Jane never received the recognition she deserved during her lifetime, the writings of Jane and her family members helped preserve Ojibwe songs and stories for future generations. Her writings have been included in several books, giving more people the chance to read her poems and stories.

In her 1838 poem
"Lines Written at Castle Island,
Lake Superior," Jane wrote,

"Here in my native inland sea
From pain and sickness would I flee
And from its shores and island bright
Gather a store of sweet delight."

EXPLORE MORE!

Some of the stories Henry Rowe Schoolcraft learned from Jane and her family later became inspiration for Henry Wadsworth Longfellow's famous poem *The Song of Hiawatha*.

MARIE LOUISE BOTTINEAU BALDWIN

(1863–1952)

Marie Louise Bottineau Baldwin was an attorney, an **advocate** for the rights of Native peoples, and a **suffragist**.

Marie was born in Pembina, North Dakota, in 1863. She was born into the Turtle Mountain Band of Chippewa Indians. She came from a family with a long history of political involvement. Her father and her grandfather were known as advocates for Turtle Mountain. Marie's family moved to Minneapolis when she was a child, and she later worked as a law clerk in her father's office.

In the 1890s, she moved to Washington, DC, to work with her father on an important **treaty rights** case for Turtle Mountain. The U.S. government refused to pay Turtle Mountain a fair price for their land.

Marie started working for the Office of Indian Affairs (OIA, now the **Bureau of Indian Affairs**) in 1904, and she spent 30 years with the organization. She believed this job would give her the chance to improve conditions for Native peoples. She was able to meet with Native **activists** from across the country, and what she learned from their experiences helped shape her work at the OIA.

Marie's father died in 1911 when Marie was nearly 50 years old. Her father's death inspired her to enroll at the Washington College of Law. She was the first Native student—and the first woman of color—to graduate from the college. She was also a suffragist and advocated for women's right to vote.

In 1911, Marie was invited to speak at a conference that was organized by the Society of American Indians (SAI). SAI was the first Native rights organization created by Native people. Marie was elected treasurer of the SAI in 1915. She worked with other Native people to support Native rights issues and to combat **stereotypes**.

Marie retired from the Office of Indian Affairs in 1932. She moved to Los Angeles in 1949 and passed away in 1952. She was 88 years old. She had spent her life advocating for Native people and celebrating Native traditions, histories, and cultures.

Few of Marie's writings have survived, but some quotes have been preserved. In a speech from 1911, she noted that, in many Native nations, a woman was "on an absolute equality with her sons and brothers."

EXPLORE MORE!

To learn more about the history of women's rights, check out *Bold Women in History: 15 Women's Rights Activists You Should Know*, by Meghan Vestal.

SUSAN LA FLESCHE PICOTTE

(1865–1915)

Susan La Flesche Picotte was the first Native American to earn a medical degree, and she was the first Native woman to work as a physician.

Susan was born on the Omaha **Reservation** in Nebraska in 1865. Her father, Joseph, was one of the leaders of the Omaha nation. Her mother, Mary, was the daughter of a U.S. Army surgeon. When Susan was only 8 years old, she watched a white doctor refuse to help a sick Native woman. Susan couldn't understand why the doctor wouldn't help someone who was sick. She decided to become a doctor and help people on the reservation.

But it wasn't easy. Many people didn't believe that women could be doctors. Even fewer thought that a Native woman could be a doctor. Susan proved them all wrong. She went to medical school at the Women's Medical College of Pennsylvania. At the age of 24, she became the first Native American—man or woman—to earn a medical degree.

Susan moved back to the Omaha Reservation. She started working as the doctor at the boarding school on the reservation, but people from all across the reservation came to her for help. People on the Omaha Reservation suffered from diseases such as tuberculosis, measles, and the flu. She set up her own office on the reservation to treat patients.

Susan was more than just a doctor for the Omaha people. She started a library, and she translated legal documents. She went to Washington, DC, to advocate for her people. She collected enough money to build a hospital on the reservation. She dedicated her life to the health and welfare of her people, and she saved countless lives along the way. Susan helped as many people as she could until she died in 1915 at the age of 50.

"I don't want to grow old and quiet before my time."

EXPLORE MORE!

The hospital Susan built in 1913 still exists! Today it offers medical care, cultural events, and programs for young people.

ANGEL DE CORA

(c. 1870–1919)

Angel De Cora was a Winnebago painter, illustrator, and teacher. She also advocated for the rights of Native people.

Angel was born on the Winnebago Reservation in Nebraska in the late 1860s or early 1870s. Her father was the son of a respected Winnebago leader, and her mother had French ancestry. She and her family spent their summers on the reservation and their winters in the forests along the rivers. Her Winnebago name, Hinook-Mahiwi-Kalinaka, means "Fleecy Clouds Floating in Space."

When Angel was about 13, she and several other children were taken from the reservation and forced to go to a **federal Indian boarding school**. The U.S. government had set up schools across the country with the goal of destroying Native languages and cultures. Some Native people sent their children to these schools so they could learn to navigate American society, but others wanted to keep their children at home. Angel was taken to the Hampton Institute in Virginia, which was more than a thousand miles away from her home on the reservation. Years later, she wrote about how worried her mother must have been when she realized her daughter was missing.

At Hampton, Angel realized how much she loved art. It helped her feel a little less homesick. Angel continued to study art. Her paintings and illustrations combined traditional Native elements with the techniques she learned in school.
Her illustrations appeared in books and magazines.

In 1906, Angel established the Native art department at the Carlisle Indian Industrial School, and she taught her students to embrace their Native heritage in their work. She supported Native students at boarding schools and helped them use art to understand what had happened to them.

Like Zitkala-Ša, Marie Louise Bottineau Baldwin, and Laura Cornelius Kellogg, Angel was a founding member of the Society of American Indians, which was created in 1911.

Angel died in 1919. During her life, she advocated for Native art, Native artists, and Native rights. She gave papers and lectures, and she participated in major art exhibitions around the country.

"I have taken care to leave my pupils' creative faculty absolutely independent and to let each student draw from his own mind, true to his own thought."

EXPLORE MORE!

The Angel De Cora Museum and Research Center supports the history, art, and culture of the Winnebago Tribe of Nebraska.

ZITKALA-ŠA

(1876–1938)

Zitkala-Ša was a Yankton Dakota teacher, musician, speaker, and activist.

Zitkala-Ša was born on the Yankton Reservation in South Dakota in 1876. Her name means "Red Bird" in Dakota. Missionaries came to the reservation when she was only 8 years old. They convinced several children—including Zitkala-Ša—to leave the reservation for a boarding school. Her mother did not want her to go, but the missionaries took her anyway. She later wrote about the experience, explaining how the teachers at the school held her down and cut off her hair.

Like many Native children in the late nineteenth and early twentieth centuries, Zitkala-Ša wasn't sure where she belonged. After leaving school, she didn't feel at home on the reservation. At these boarding schools, teachers would not let the children speak their native languages. Because of this, many forgot their languages. Once they returned home, they couldn't communicate with their families. Three years later, Zitkala-Ša decided to continue her education off the reservation. She studied music and became a music teacher.

In 1900, she took a trip back to her reservation. She was shocked by what she saw. Her family's home needed repairs, and many people lived in poverty. Even worse, settlers had moved onto the lands that had been reserved for Native people. She started writing about what she saw because she wanted people to know about the poor conditions Native people faced on reservations.

Like Marie Louise Bottineau Baldwin and Angel De Cora, Zitkala-Ša joined the Society of American Indians. She served as its secretary, and in 1918 she became the editor of its *American Indian Magazine*. She wrote letters to the Office of Indian Affairs (now the Bureau of Indian Affairs) criticizing their treatment of Native people. She gave lectures across the country in support of traditional Native cultures. She co-founded the National Council of American Indians in 1926.

Zitkala-Ša died in 1938. Her traumatic experiences as a child had shaped the rest of her life. She used her platform to educate people about Native issues. The work she did helped pave the way for generations of Native activists and advocates. While her husband, Raymond, struggled to keep the National Council of American Indians going after she died, their work inspired the 1944 creation of the National Congress of American Indians. It's the largest and oldest organization that supports Native American and Alaska Native rights.

"Even nature seemed to have no place for me."

EXPLORE MORE!

Zitkala-Ša co-wrote an opera titled *The Sun Dance Opera*. She combined her classical musical training with traditional aspects of Native culture and history.

LAURA CORNELIUS KELLOGG

(1880–1947)

Laura Cornelius Kellogg was an Oneida author, speaker, activist, and leader.

Laura was born on the Oneida Reservation in Wisconsin in 1880. She came from a long line of Oneida leaders. One of her grandfathers, Chief Daniel Bread, had helped the Oneida people find a new homeland after they were forcibly removed from their traditional lands in New York. Laura attended an Episcopal school as a child, but she also stayed connected to the traditional teachings of the Oneida.

Laura spent her life fighting to protect Native ways of life. She testified before the United States Senate. She worked as a teacher at a federal Indian boarding school in California. She advocated for Native rights at the League of Nations in Switzerland. She called on the government to be held accountable for ignoring the treaties it had made with Native nations such as the Oneida. She argued for women's rights.

Laura was also one of the founders of the Society of American Indians. It was the first Native rights organization created by—and for—Native people. Laura served as the first secretary of the organization. She was an accomplished speaker, and she pushed for better policies for Native nations. She wanted to improve economic opportunities on reservations.

While Laura's advocacy for Native people earned the respect of many of her colleagues, others disagreed with her. Some Native activists called her a "visionary" and a "woman of brilliance," but others called her "a cyclone." Today, Laura is remembered as a fierce advocate for Native rights and Native nations.

"To do something great when I grew up was impressed upon me from my cradle by my parents, and I have known no other ambition."

EXPLORE MORE!

In the 1820s, the Oneida were forced to move from New York to what is now the state of Wisconsin. A **treaty** in 1838 established the borders of their new reservation in Wisconsin.

* OLIVIA POOLE *

(1889–1975)

Susan Olivia Poole (known as Olivia Poole) was an Indigenous inventor and **entrepreneur**. She's credited with inventing the baby jumper known as the Jolly Jumper.

Olivia was born in Devils Lake, North Dakota, in 1889. She grew up on the White Earth Reservation in northern Minnesota. As a child, she saw Ojibwe mothers use what they called a *dikinaagan*, or a cradleboard. A mother would wrap her baby in a cloth, set the baby in the *dikinaagan*, and securely fasten the straps. Mothers could strap the *dikinaagan* to their backs or lean them upright. Sometimes mothers would bounce the babies in the *dikinaagan* like they were on a swing or a hammock.

Olivia studied music at Brandon College (now Brandon University) in Manitoba, Canada. She met her husband in Manitoba, and they later moved to Ontario. Olivia had her first child in 1910. She remembered how Ojibwe mothers used the *dikinaagan* to soothe their babies. She didn't have one of her own, so she sewed a cloth diaper into a harness. She made a brace out of an old axe handle. She added a spring so the baby could bounce on its own. She called it a Jolly Jumper.

Olivia used her Jolly Jumper with all seven of her children. She kept working on the design as her children had their own children. The jumpers worked so well that her family told her she should try to sell them! The Jolly Jumpers became available for purchase in the early 1950s.

She applied for a patent in 1957. Owning a patent meant having exclusive rights to make and sell her invention. She and her son Joseph created Poole Manufacturing Co. Ltd. The Poole family sold the business in the 1960s.

Olivia died of complications from pneumonia in 1975. She was one of the first Native women in Canada to patent an invention, and she drew on Native history to make it happen.

A Jolly Jumper ad from the 1960s said that it could be put up in almost any doorway—or "outdoors on a tree."

EXPLORE MORE!

Today, the Jolly Jumper brand still sells all kinds of products for babies.

* MARY SULLY *

(1896–1963)

Mary Sully was a Yankton Dakota artist. She was known for combining modern art techniques with traditional Native elements.

When she was born, her parents named her Susan Mabel Deloria. She was born on the Standing Rock Reservation in South Dakota in 1896. Her father, Philip J. Deloria, was active in the Episcopal Church community on the reservation. Her mother was the child of an army officer and a Native woman. Her mother's Native name was Akíčtawiŋ, or "Soldier Woman," and she was also known as Mary Sully, a name that Susan would later adopt.

Mary was always very shy. She took a few art classes, but she was mostly self-taught. Mary usually worked with ink and colored pencils. She created close to 200 drawings during her life, and her older sister kept them in a cardboard box among her own papers and writings. Mary's drawings were usually created in sets of three. She was inspired by modern geometric art as well as Native quilting, beadwork, and quillwork. She also created "personality prints" of famous people such as Thomas Edison and Babe Ruth.

Mary died in 1963, and her artwork was nearly lost forever. Her collection of drawings first went to her older sister and then to her younger brother. Her brother gave them to his daughter-in-law, Barbara, who happened to be a librarian. Barbara hid them in a suitcase under a stairwell. It wasn't until 2006 that Barbara and her son found them and realized that Mary had been an incredible artist.

Mary spent most of her life as a relatively unknown artist. She didn't give interviews, write letters, or keep a diary. But today, Mary's artwork has been on display across the country. The Metropolitan Museum of Art now holds most of her artwork in its collection, and Mary is finally getting the recognition she always deserved.

According to her great-nephew, Philip J. Deloria, Mary Sully was "a solo artist in every sense of the word."

EXPLORE MORE!

Mary's older sister, Ella Cara Deloria, became a famous scholar. She wrote a novel called *Waterlily*.

SUSIE WALKING BEAR YELLOWTAIL

(1903–1981)

Susie Walking Bear Yellowtail was a public health advocate for Native people. She was also the first Apsáalooke (Crow) person to become a registered nurse.

Susie was born in 1903 in Montana. Both of her parents died when she was young. Like many other Native children, she was sent to boarding school. She attended several schools, and she later enrolled in the School of Nursing at Boston City Hospital. After graduating with honors in 1923, she trained at a hospital in Massachusetts. In 1927, she became the first Apsáalooke registered nurse—and one of the first Native registered nurses in the country.

Susie went back to her reservation to work at the hospital. The hospital was run by the Indian Health Service, which is part of the federal government. Everywhere she went, she saw Native people struggling with health conditions. She saw non-Native doctors and nurses who didn't understand Apsáalooke culture and ways of life. She saw Apsáalooke children dying from a lack of access to medical care. She saw that Apsáalooke elders couldn't always communicate with doctors.

Susie started advocating for Apsáalooke people, and she created an outreach program for reservations. She pushed the Indian Health Service to let traditional healers work with Native patients. These healers often used traditional Apsáalooke prayers, songs, and medicines to care for sick people. Having access to their traditional methods often helped Apsáalooke people feel better about being in the hospital. She also served as a **midwife** for Apsáalooke women. She believed that better medical care would lead to better living conditions for Native people.

Susie died in 1981, but her legacy lives on. She had blazed a trail for Native health care. She had helped create the American Indian Nurses Association in the 1970s. The organization advocated for Native health and recruited young Native women to work as nurses. Today, many Native health practitioners draw on the same practices Susie pioneered many decades ago.

"The Indians' needs are many, but most urgent is the need for better education."

EXPLORE MORE!

Did you know that Native women such as Cora Elm (Oneida) and Marcella LeBeau (Lakota) served overseas as nurses during World War I and World War II?

✳ MAUDE KEGG ✳

(1904–1996)

Maude Kegg was a Mille Lacs Ojibwe writer, artist, and cultural interpreter. As a cultural interpreter, she helped teach people about Ojibwe history and culture.

Maude was born at her family's wild rice camp in Crow Wing County, Minnesota. She was born sometime in the late summer of 1904. Her family didn't follow the Western calendar system, so she later chose August 26 as the day to celebrate her birthday. Her parents named her Naawakamigookwe [Naah-wah-kah-mih-goo-kway], which means "Middle of the Earth Woman." Maude's mother died when Maude was just a baby, so her grandmother helped care for her and teach her.

As a child, Maude spent her winters going to school and the rest of the year following the traditional cycles of the Ojibwe. In the spring, she and her family stayed at their sugar bush camp. They harvested sap from maple trees to make maple sugar and maple syrup. In the summer, they fished and gardened. In the fall, they gathered wild rice.

In the 1920s, Maude served as a translator for the owners of the Mille Lacs Trading Post. Because she spoke both English and Ojibwe, she was able to communicate with the Ojibwe people who came to the trading post, a small store where people could shop for goods they needed. She later started working at the trading post museum, and she sold her beadwork, handmade moccasins, and other crafts. When the owners of the trading post donated their collections to the Minnesota Historical Society, Maude kept working at the museum as a cultural interpreter. As a cultural interpreter, Maude helped teach museum visitors about Ojibwe history and culture. She was famous for her beadwork. Some of her pieces are even in the Smithsonian!

In the 1970s, Maude was worried that Ojibwe people might not remember their history and culture. She started dictating stories that other people wrote down and turned into books to make sure the histories wouldn't be forgotten.

Maude died in 1996. She had spent her life following Ojibwe traditions and helping make sure Ojibwe people—and non-Ojibwe people—understood the importance of Native history, art, and culture.

Maude learned a lot about Ojibwe history and culture from her grandmother: "I don't know how to write it, but she didn't write it either. She just told me the things which I remember."

EXPLORE MORE!

In 1986, the governor of Minnesota proclaimed August 26 to be Mrs. Maude Kegg Day, in honor of "her many years of knowledge, wisdom, and efforts in the preservation of Ojibwe culture and language."

BERTHA PARKER

(1907–1978)

Bertha Parker is considered the first Native woman to work as an archaeologist. An archaeologist studies human history by digging into the ground at important sites and looking for **artifacts** such as bones, tools, or pieces of buildings.

Bertha was born in New York in 1907. It's been said that she was born in a tent near an archaeological excavation site. Her father was Seneca, and his name was Arthur C. Parker. He was an archaeologist, and he served as the first president of the Society for American Archaeology. He was also a founding member of the Society of American Indians alongside other activists like Marie Louise Bottineau Baldwin and Zitkala-Ša.

As a child, Bertha often went on archaeological excavations with her father. Her parents divorced when she was 7, and she and her mother, who was an actress, moved to Los Angeles. As a teenager, Bertha acted in Hollywood films and performed with the Ringling Brothers and Barnum & Bailey circuses. Her uncle was also an archaeologist and an anthropologist, and in 1929 he and his family gave Bertha a place to stay. In exchange, Bertha would work as the cook, secretary, and assistant archaeologist on his excavations.

While she never received formal training, she learned how to be an archaeologist by working in the field. Bertha was part of some of the biggest discoveries of the twentieth century. In the 1930s, she made a groundbreaking discovery at Gypsum Cave in Nevada. She put on a mask and a headlamp, then slid through a small opening that the others on the team couldn't fit through. Bertha found the skull of an extinct giant ground sloth next to some tools humans had made thousands of years ago. At the time, this was the earliest record of humans in North America. Bertha's discovery made headlines in newspapers across the country, and she became well known as the first Native woman to work as an archaeologist.

Bertha continued to make important archaeological discoveries throughout her career. She also worked at the Southwest Museum in Los Angeles, California, and published several stories and articles throughout her career. Unfortunately, few accounts actually credited her by name—most referred to her as someone's wife, daughter, or niece. When Bertha died in 1978, the plaque where she was buried was inscribed only with her married name, Mrs. Iron Eyes Cody. Recently, though, more and more people have started to recognize her name and celebrate her many achievements.

"I have met so many lovely people of the scientific world, that I have learned quite a lot, they are all so nice to me, that I am very happy in my work, and the hard knocks make me appreciate it all the more."

EXPLORE MORE!

The Southwest Museum is the oldest museum in Los Angeles.

MARY GOLDA ROSS

(1908–2008)

Mary Golda Ross was the first Native American woman to work as an engineer. She's best known for her work in the field of aerospace engineering.

Mary was born in Park Hill, Oklahoma, in 1908. Her family was Cherokee. Cherokee tradition advocates for girls to have the same access to education that boys do. Mary's parents sent her to live with her grandparents in Tahlequah, Oklahoma, when she was little. They wanted to make sure she got the best education she could. Mary loved math. She graduated with a degree in mathematics in 1928 and went on to earn a master's degree.

Mary worked for the Office of Indian Affairs. She also worked at a school in New Mexico. When the United States entered World War II in 1941, thousands of Americans joined the war effort. Mary moved to California to look for work. She was hired by the Lockheed Aircraft Corporation as a mathematical research assistant in 1942. She helped fix problems with fighter planes. In 1950, she became Lockheed's first woman engineer.

In 1953, Lockheed asked 40 engineers to work on a top-secret project. Mary was the only woman on the team. She was also the only Native person in the group. These engineers worked on plans for satellites and space travel. Mary also worked on missiles and reentry vehicles. Reentry vehicles are spacecrafts or parts of missiles that are designed to return to Earth after they've been in orbit or in outer space. Mary worked with NASA and helped write about the possibilities of space travel to other planets.

Mary retired in 1973. She gave speeches about education, inspiring women and Native people to study math and engineering. Mary Golda Ross died shortly before what would have been her 100th birthday. A lot of her work is still classified. That means it's kept secret by the government, so it's hard to know just how much she contributed to science. But it's important to celebrate who she was as an engineer and as a Native woman.

"Math was more fun than anything else. It was always a game to me."

EXPLORE MORE!

You can learn more about Mary Golda Ross at the First Americans Museum in Oklahoma.

✳ ANNIE DODGE WAUNEKA ✳

(1910–1997)

Annie Dodge Wauneka was a Diné (Navajo) leader and public health advocate. She was also the first Native American to receive the Presidential Medal of Freedom.

Annie was born in Arizona in 1910. She was born into the Tse níjikíní (Cliff Dwelling People) clan. Her father was a well-known Diné leader. As a child, she helped herd sheep and tend to her family's livestock. She was 8 years old when she was sent to a reservation school. That same year, an influenza epidemic tore through the Navajo Nation reservation. As one of the few children who survived, Annie helped care for other people who were suffering.

She decided she wanted to study medicine and help her people. She studied public health at the University of Arizona. Her goal was to make sure that Native people could have clean homes and clean water. In 1951, she was one of the first women elected to the Navajo Nation Council. She also led the council's Health and Welfare Committee. Annie encouraged officials to allow Diné children to be educated closer to their homes and their families, instead of being sent to faraway boarding schools.

Annie encouraged doctors to learn more about their Diné patients' beliefs and values. She wrote a medical dictionary in English and Diné so doctors and patients could better communicate with each other. She hosted a radio show in Diné to share information about disease prevention and treatment, which helped stop the spread of diseases such as tuberculosis. Annie also helped improve housing and sanitation conditions on the reservation.

Annie Dodge Wauneka died in 1997. She had spent years traveling around the reservation and across the country to advocate for Diné people. She had traveled to Washington, DC, to testify before government committees. People all over the United States recognized the importance of her work, and her legacy lives on today.

"I'll go and do more."

EXPLORE MORE!

Annie Dodge Wauneka was also a Girl Scout leader!

ELIZABETH PERATROVICH

(1911–1958)

Elizabeth Wanamaker Peratrovich was a Tlingit civil rights activist. She advocated for the rights of Alaska Native people.

Elizabeth was born in 1911 in an Alaska fishing community called Petersburg. Her mother was Tlingit, and her father was Irish. Her parents weren't able to take care of her, so she was adopted by a couple who lived in Sitka. Her adoptive parents spoke both English and Tlingit, so Elizabeth learned both languages. They spent their summers fishing for salmon, digging for clams, and picking berries.

As she grew older, Elizabeth noticed that Alaska Native people weren't welcome in schools, hospitals, or movie theaters the way white people were. Businesses posted signs on their doors and windows that said "No Natives Allowed." Alaska Native people like Elizabeth's father came together to fight this **discrimination**. They formed the Alaska Native Brotherhood (ANB) in 1912 and the Alaska Native Sisterhood (ANS) in 1914.

Elizabeth and her husband, Roy Peratrovich, joined the ANB and the ANS. When they moved to Juneau, they couldn't find good homes to rent. Their children had to go to a different school. Elizabeth fought for Alaska Native children to be able to go to white schools. Elizabeth and Roy helped draft an anti-discrimination bill that went to the Alaska Territorial Legislature in 1943. If the bill was passed, Alaska Native people would have protection against discrimination. They would be able to shop, live, and go to school where they wanted to. But the legislature voted it down.

Elizabeth refused to give up. She spent the next two years traveling throughout southeastern Alaska to build support for the bill. She told Alaska Native people how the bill could help them. Finally, in 1945, the legislature passed the bill. The Alaska Equal Rights Act was the first anti-discrimination act in the nation!

Elizabeth was only 47 when she died in 1958, but her legacy lives on in the history of the fight for civil rights.

"This is a step in the right direction, and we will continue in our endeavors to obtain, for our people, rights enjoyed by all."

EXPLORE MORE!

Alaska celebrates Elizabeth Peratrovich Day every February 16, the day the governor signed the anti-discrimination act into law.

OLA MILDRED REXROAT

(1917–2017)

Ola Mildred Rexroat was an Oglala Lakota military pilot. She was the only Native woman to serve in the Women Airforce Service Pilots (WASP) program.

Known as Millie, Ola Rexroat was born in Kansas in 1917. Her mother was Oglala Lakota. Her father worked for newspapers. Growing up, Millie's family moved all over the country. But they also spent a lot of time with her grandma on the Pine Ridge Reservation in South Dakota.

Millie graduated from the University of New Mexico in 1939. She took a job at the Army War College in Washington, DC. But everything changed when the United States entered World War II.

Millie wanted to serve her country. She wanted to join the Marine Corps, so she sent them a telegram asking how she could join. But they didn't think women should serve. She started taking flying lessons at a local airport and applied to the WASP program for women pilots. More than 25,000 women applied. Millie was one of only around 1,000 who completed the training. She was also the only Native woman to serve as a WASP.

Millie flew planes that carried important supplies and members of the military. She towed targets so that student gunners could practice their aim. But when the war ended, so did the WASP program. There weren't any options for women to serve as pilots outside the military. Women like Millie wouldn't be able to fly again in the military for several decades. So Millie joined the Air Force. She was one of the first women to work as an air traffic controller during the Korean War. An air traffic controller guides planes to keep them organized and safe. After 10 years in the Air Force, she spent more than 30 years as an air traffic controller for the Federal Aviation Administration in Santa Fe, New Mexico.

Millie and the other WASP pilots received Congressional Gold Medals in 2009. Millie died two months before what would have been her 100th birthday. After her death, the Ellsworth Air Force Base in South Dakota named their airfield operations building after her.

“I just did what I was expected to do and tried to do it the best way I could.”

EXPLORE MORE!

The records of the WASPs were classified, or kept secret by the government, for more than 30 years. It took decades for these women to get the recognition they deserved.

IGNATIA BROKER

(1919–1987)

Ignatia Broker was an Ojibwe writer. She was also a leader in the Native community of Minneapolis, Minnesota.

Ignatia was born on the White Earth Reservation in northern Minnesota in 1919. She went to the Wahpeton Indian School in North Dakota and the Haskell Institute in Kansas. She knew what life was like on the reservation, and she also knew what life was like in a bigger city. She moved to the Twin Cities of Minneapolis and St. Paul, Minnesota, in 1941. She worked in a defense plant during World War II to support the war effort. She knew she hadn't gotten a great education in the boarding schools, so she went to night school to make up for it. Her husband served in World War II and was later killed during the Korean War.

Even though Native people like Ignatia had helped the United States win World War II, they still dealt with racism and discrimination. Ignatia advocated for Native people in the Twin Cities. She worked at the *Minneapolis Star and Tribune* newspaper, and she worked with Minneapolis Public Schools to build their Native studies curriculum. Along with other Ojibwe women, Ignatia pushed for the creation of an American Indian Center in the 1960s and 1970s.

Ignatia was also a writer. She's most well known for her 1983 nonfiction novel *Night Flying Woman*. The novel tells the story of her great-great-grandmother Ni-bo-wi-se-gwe, who was born in the mid-1800s. Also known as Oona, Ni-bo-wi-se-gwe was a child when her people were forced onto a reservation. Through the book, Ignatia describes the hardships her ancestors faced while also telling a beautiful story of survival.

In 1984, three years before she died, Ignatia was one of 14 women who were given a Wonder Woman Award in honor of their accomplishments. Ignatia died in 1987. Her legacy lives on through her writings, and it lives on through the Native community that still calls the Twin Cities home. Ignatia worked with many organizations to help support Native people, and people still read and share her writings.

"I can close my eyes and I am back in the past."

EXPLORE MORE!

The Minneapolis American Indian Center (MAIC) is one of the oldest Indian centers in the country. It was founded in 1975.

✳ GRACE THORPE ✳

(1921–2008)

Grace Thorpe was a Sac and Fox military veteran and Native rights activist. She also advocated for the environment.

Grace was born in Oklahoma in 1921. Her father was Jim Thorpe, who was considered one of the greatest athletes who'd ever lived. Her mother, Iva, had met Jim when they were both students at the Carlisle Indian Industrial School in Pennsylvania. Grace's parents divorced when she was very young, and she spent time with both parents as she was growing up. As a child, Grace went to an all-girls school in Oklahoma before attending the Haskell Institute in Kansas. Like Carlisle, Haskell was a federal Indian boarding school.

Grace wanted to serve her country when World War II began. She worked for the Ford Motor Company in 1943 before joining the Women's Army Corps (WAC). She earned the rank of corporal after completing her training. She worked as a recruiter before being sent overseas in 1944. She served in New Guinea, the Philippines, and Japan.

After the war, she spent the rest of her life advocating for Native rights and Native people—including her father. Jim Thorpe had won two gold medals in the 1912 Olympic Games, but they'd been taken away in 1913 after people learned that he'd spent a couple of summers playing baseball semi-professionally, which was against the rules. Grace was among the many people who thought her father deserved to keep his Olympic medals. She spent decades trying to get his legacy restored. In 1983, she finally succeeded.

She later moved back to Oklahoma, and she served as a tribal judge and health commissioner. She learned that the Sac and Fox Nation, whose reservation is in Oklahoma, had allowed the government to use tribal lands for nuclear testing. Grace believed the government was taking advantage of Native nations. She believed the government was hiding the fact that the tests could have harmful effects. These tests could make people sick, contaminate the environment, and have deadly impacts on wildlife. Grace worked to stop harmful nuclear waste from being stored on reservations. She died in 2008, and she is remembered for serving her country and fighting for Native rights.

"I should be working for my people."

EXPLORE MORE!

Grace earned a Bronze Star for her military service in the Battle of New Guinea.

BETTY MAE TIGER JUMPER

(1923–2011)

Betty Mae Tiger Jumper was the first Seminole person to graduate from high school, the first Seminole nurse, and the first woman to lead the Seminole Tribe of Florida.

Betty Mae was born in Indiantown, Florida, in 1923. Her mother was Seminole, and her father was white. It wasn't always easy for Betty Mae and her brother. There weren't many Seminole kids who also had one white parent, so it was hard for them to fit in. Her family, hoping things would be better away from the reservation, moved closer to Fort Lauderdale when Betty Mae was about 5 years old. Her mother got a job picking beans and tomatoes, and Betty Mae and her brother helped.

Seminole kids like Betty Mae weren't allowed to go to schools with white students. They also couldn't go to segregated schools for Black children, so she didn't have any chance for an education. But when she was 14, Betty Mae convinced her family to let her go to a boarding school in North Carolina. She knew she could get a better education in North Carolina than she could in Florida, and she wanted to find a way to help her people. In 1949, she and her cousin became the first Seminole students to graduate from high school.

Betty Mae saw how many Seminole children died from diseases that could be cured, so she went to nursing school in Oklahoma. She was the first Seminole person to become a nurse. Betty Mae worked to improve health care, housing, education, and living conditions on the Seminole Reservation. She was elected to the tribal council in 1957, and 10 years later she was elected chairwoman. Betty Mae spent her time on the council working to improve health care, education, and housing for the Seminole.

Betty Mae Tiger Jumper remains the only Seminole woman to be elected to chair the tribal council. When she left office, she oversaw the publication of the first Seminole newspaper—which is still published today. She died in 2011, and she continues to be celebrated for the work she did for the Seminole people.

> “I am deeply grateful for the education I have received and I want sincerely to use it in the interests of my people.”

EXPLORE MORE!

The Seminole call themselves “the Unconquered People” because their ancestors never surrendered to the American military.

MINNIE SPOTTED WOLF

(1923–1987)

Minnie Spotted Wolf was one of the first Native women to serve in the Marine Corps Women's Reserve. She served in the military during and after World War II.

Minnie was Blackfeet. She was born near Heart Butte, Montana, and grew up on a ranch. She learned how to cut fence posts, drive trucks, and get horses tame enough to ride. She later said that Marine Corps boot camp was hard, but it wasn't too bad compared to how she'd grown up.

Like Grace Thorpe and many other Native women, Minnie wanted to serve her country when the United States entered World War II. When the war began, government and military officials realized they needed both men and women to help win the war. The Marine Corps Women's Reserve was formed in 1943. Minnie was one of the first Native women to enlist. She spent four years as a heavy-equipment operator, and she also served as a driver on military bases in Hawaii and California. During the war, heavy-equipment operators would use bulldozers, graders, and other machines to build roads and maintain airfields.

Minnie went back to Montana after she was discharged from the military in 1947. She went to college and earned degrees in elementary education. She spent nearly 30 years as a teacher. She still loved riding horses, and her daughter proudly remembered how Minnie could still outride many men. Minnie died in 1987 and was buried in her military uniform. In 2019, a section of Montana highway was named in her honor.

> “When it was over, I was proud of myself and all that I had accomplished.”

EXPLORE MORE!

Minnie was featured in a 1940s comic book that promoted the war effort.

* MARIA TALLCHIEF *

(1925–2013)

Maria Tallchief was an Osage ballet dancer. She was the first Native prima ballerina and also the first American prima ballerina.

Maria was born Elizabeth Marie Tall Chief on the Osage Nation reservation in Oklahoma. Her family called her Betty Marie. Her father was Osage, and her mother was Scots-Irish. Her sister, Marjorie, was born in 1926. Both sisters started taking dance lessons in 1930. Their mother wanted the girls to be famous dancers, so she moved the family to California in 1933. The girls loved to dance. They studied under several famous teachers, and Betty Marie joined the Ballet Russe de Monte Carlo in 1942 after she finished high school.

The Ballet Russe was one of the most well-known ballet companies in the world. Most of the famous ballet dancers came from Russia. The Ballet Russe told Betty Marie she should change her name to Maria Tallchieva to sound more Russian. She wanted to keep her Osage name, so she became Maria Tallchief. But people in the world of ballet weren't used to seeing Native dancers on stage. Sometimes newspaper writers focused more on the color of her skin than the quality of her dancing.

In 1942, a man named George Balanchine started creating dances for the Ballet Russe. George formed a ballet company in 1946, and today it's known as the New York City Ballet. Maria became one of the leading stars of the company. George created some of the most famous roles just for her, like the Firebird in *The Firebird* and the Sugar Plum Fairy in *The Nutcracker*. In 1947, Maria was named prima ballerina, which is the highest possible rank for a ballet dancer. She was the first American—and Native—prima ballerina.

Maria helped make ballet popular in America. Even though she retired from the stage in 1965, she spent the rest of her life teaching and directing ballet. She and her sister, Marjorie, created a ballet company in Chicago, and she received many honors and awards during her life. She died in 2013 at the age of 88. She's been honored by the Osage Nation, and she's still remembered for the impact she left on the world of ballet.

“As long as I live, I’ll never forget the roar,” Maria once wrote of the sound of the audience after her first performance as the Firebird.

EXPLORE MORE!

The Nutcracker is one of the most popular ballets in the world. Every year, more than 100,000 people see the New York City Ballet’s performance.

✳ ALBERTA SCHENCK ✳

(1928–2009)

Alberta Schenck was an Iñupiaq activist. She spoke out against the unfair treatment of Alaska Natives, and her experiences helped shape the Alaska Equal Rights Act of 1945.

Alberta was born in Nome, Alaska, in 1928. Alaska was still a U.S. **territory** at the time. Her father was a World War I veteran, and her mother was Iñupiaq. Alaska Native people faced harassment, segregation, and discrimination. It was common for hotels and restaurants to say they wouldn't serve Alaska Native people. Alaska Native children had to go to separate schools.

In 1944, Alberta was a teenager working as an usher at a movie theater in Nome. Part of her job included making sure that Alaska Native people didn't sit in the "whites only" section of the theater. She didn't think it was fair that the movie theater had separate seating sections. She spoke out against the policy and lost her job.

But Alberta didn't back down. She wrote an essay about her experience that was published in the local newspaper. People started paying attention to what was happening. When she was invited to go to the movies with a white army sergeant, they sat in the "whites only" section of the theater. Alberta was arrested, and she was forced to spend the night in jail.

Alberta's experience inspired Alaska Native activists such as Elizabeth Peratrovich. Alaska Native people bought tickets for movies and sat wherever they wanted. Politicians used Alberta's story to encourage the members of the Alaska Territorial Legislature to pass an anti-discrimination act. This meant that Alaska Native people could sit wherever they wanted to in a movie theater. They could go in any stores they wanted to, and they wouldn't have to go to different schools. People never forgot about Alberta's fight for civil rights, and in 2011 she was inducted into the Alaska Women's Hall of Fame.

In her essay that was published in the *Nome Nugget*, Alberta wrote, “I believe we Americans and also our Allies are fighting for the purpose of freedom.”

EXPLORE MORE!

In honor of her activism, Alberta was crowned “the Queen of Nome” during the city’s 1944 spring carnival.

MARIA PEARSON

(1932–2003)

Maria Pearson was a Native activist. She advocated for laws that would respect Native remains, protect Native graves, and return stolen items and ancestors to Native nations.

Maria was born in South Dakota in 1932. Her mother gave her the Yankton name Hai-Mecha Eunka, which means "Running Moccasin." Maria learned about Yankton Dakota traditions and customs from her grandma, and these teachings would stay with her throughout her life.

In 1971, Maria's husband told her that the Iowa Department of Transportation (DOT) had uncovered nearly 30 skeletons during road construction. The DOT had quickly reburied the skeletons of the 26 white people who had been found. Instead of treating the Native skeletons—including a mother and child—with the same respect, the DOT sent them to the Office of the State Archaeologist to be studied.

Dressed in her **regalia**, Maria went to the capitol building and demanded to talk to the governor. She wanted him to know that it was wrong to treat the remains of Native people like this. He was shocked to hear what had happened, and Maria's advocacy led to the first law that would help protect Native ancestors. It was passed in 1976. Maria's actions inspired other people across the country. Thanks to people like Maria, Congress passed the Native American Graves Protection and Repatriation Act (NAGPRA) in 1990. This law protects Native burial sites and objects. It also requires museums to return artifacts and objects to Native nations.

Maria spent the rest of her life working to make sure that Native people, Native remains, and Native graves were treated with respect. She served on a number of committees throughout Iowa, and she was recognized for her leadership. She helped build relationships between the governor's office and Native people. Maria died in 2003, and she's remembered for fighting for the rights of Native people in Iowa and across the country.

"You can give me back my people's bones and you can quit digging them up," Maria told the governor of Iowa.

EXPLORE MORE!

The National Museum of the American Indian opened on the National Mall in Washington, DC, in 2004. It holds one of the largest collections of Native artifacts in the world.

JANET McCLOUD

(1934–2003)

Janet McCloud was a Tulalip activist. She helped lead a movement in the Pacific Northwest to uphold the treaty rights of Native nations.

Janet was born on the Tulalip Reservation in Washington state. Her Tulalip name, Yet-Si-Blue, means "The Woman Who Talks." Her family moved around a lot when she was a child. Because of this, she didn't learn much about Tulalip customs and traditions. She married a Nisqually man named Don McCloud, and they moved closer to the Nisqually Reservation in Washington state. Don wanted to help Native nations start their own fisheries.

Native nations such as the Nisqually had signed treaties with the U.S. government in the 1850s that protected their rights to hunt and fish. But state officials often arrested Native people for fishing—including some of Janet's relatives. Janet and Don helped create the Survival of American Indians Association. The organization helped set up what they called "fish-ins" in the 1960s. Like the "sit-in" protests in the American South, these peaceful protests helped bring attention to the issues Native people faced.

The Native protesters wanted to demonstrate peacefully. But sometimes state officials responded with violence, even attacking women and children who were participating in the protests. Janet wrote a newsletter called *Survival News* to let people know what was happening. Native people kept fighting to protect their right to fish throughout the 1960s and 1970s. In 1974, a judge finally upheld their right to fish.

Janet didn't stop there. In 1974, she helped create an organization called Women of All Red Nations (WARN). Alongside Lorelei DeCora Means, Madonna Thunder Hawk, and Phyllis Young, WARN brought almost 200 women together for its first meeting in South Dakota. They advocated for education, health care and family care, and the rights of Native women across the country. Janet died in 2003, and she's remembered for her bravery in the face of violence and intimidation.

"Our people have fought and died for these United States and we have an agreement with it to fish these grounds. We plan to do so."

EXPLORE MORE!

Want to learn more? Check out "The Fish Wars: Strategies for Taking Action," an interactive online lesson from the National Museum of the American Indian.

ADA DEER

(1935–2023)

Ada Deer was a Menominee activist and leader. She was the first Menominee to go to college and the first to get a master's degree.

Ada was born on the Menominee Reservation in Wisconsin in 1935. Her father, Joe, was Menominee, and her mother, Constance (known as Connie), was white. Her father had gone to boarding school, and her mother had worked as a nurse. Ada's family moved to Milwaukee when she was 6, but they came back to the reservation after World War II. Ada and her siblings faced a lot of racism and discrimination. When Ada was young, her mother's father tried to convince Connie to leave her husband and children. Connie refused, and Ada never forgot that experience with her grandfather.

Ada graduated from high school in 1953, and she went to college at the University of Wisconsin. At the same time, the government wanted to "terminate" the Menominee. This meant that the Menominee would lose their status as a Native nation. Many people on the reservation—including Ada's mother—believed the government wanted to steal Menominee lands and resources.

The government terminated the Menominee in 1961. Within a few years, Menominee people no longer had access to good jobs, good housing, or good health care. Ada wanted to help people on the reservation, so she earned a master's degree in social work. She also joined an organization of Menominee people who wanted to restore their government. Thanks to the advocacy of people like Ada, the Menominee were restored in 1972. In 1974, Ada became the first woman to lead the Menominee.

Ada spent the rest of her life teaching and advocating for the rights of Native people across the nation. She served in the Bureau of Indian Affairs and helped make better policies for Native nations. She created innovative programs for students studying social work so they could better serve Native communities. Ada died in 2023, and she was recognized across the country for having dedicated her life to Native people.

“I want to do,
I want to be, and
I want to help.”

EXPLORE MORE!

Ada was inducted into the National Native American Hall of Fame in 2019.

JAUNE QUICK-TO-SEE SMITH

(1940–2025)

Jaune Quick-to-See Smith was an artist, curator, educator, and activist. She was a citizen of the Confederated Salish and Kootenai Tribes, and she had other ancestors who were Shoshone, Métis, and French Cree.

Jaune was born on the Flathead Reservation in Montana. Her mother left when Jaune was only 2 years old. Jaune was raised by her father, Albert, who was a horse trader. Jaune traveled with her father as he sold horses. He would draw little pictures of animals for her, and she would carry them in her pockets. Sometimes she would pick fruits and vegetables to help make money. She also loved to read.

Jaune decided to be an artist after watching a movie about a French painter. She wanted to go to college to study art. But people told her that women couldn't be artists. They told her that Native people didn't go to college. Jaune refused to give up her dreams. She knew that she could do it, and she worked hard to make it happen.

In the 1970s, Jaune was a student at the University of New Mexico. She and other Native students formed the Grey Canyon

Artists collective, which promoted and showcased the works of Native artists. They organized a traveling exhibit. Her first solo show in New York City opened soon after. It would be the first of more than 80 exhibitions of her work across the country. She often made collages, and she also made drawings and paintings. Jaune used her art to respond to events happening around the world.

Jaune passed away in 2025 at the age of 85. She had spent her life as an artist and as a curator. A curator is someone who chooses art pieces for display in museums, galleries, and exhibitions. Many of her works were inspired by her own experiences as a Native woman. Over the course of her career, she curated more than 30 shows that focused on Native art. She showed people what contemporary Native art could look like. She helped create spaces for Native artists to show their works.

"My community always comes with me."

EXPLORE MORE!

Jaune's name comes from the French word for "yellow."

SUZAN SHOWN HARJO

(1945–)

Suzan Shown Harjo is an activist, writer, and museum curator. She helps reclaim Native lands, shapes **federal Indian policies**, and fights against racist sports team mascots.

Suzan was born in El Reno, Oklahoma, in 1945. Her father was Muscogee (Creek). Her mother was Cheyenne. Suzan spent most of her childhood on her grandparents' farm. But her dad was in the U.S. Army, so the family lived for several years in Italy when he was stationed there. They came back to the United States when Suzan was 16, and Suzan graduated from high school in Oklahoma City.

Once they came back to the U.S., Suzan learned about the ongoing protests against mascots that used stereotypical or **derogatory** images of Native people. At the time, the University of Oklahoma's mascot was called "Little Red." A white student wearing red makeup and body paint would pretend to do Native dances at football games. Many Native people believed the university should find a different mascot. This helped shape

Suzan's later activism and advocacy, especially in relation to the football team now known as the Washington Commanders.

Suzan moved to New York when she was 20. She married a man named Frank Ray Harjo, and they started making radio shows together. *Seeing Red* was the first regularly scheduled Native news radio show in the country. The show included news, music, and interviews.

Suzan and Frank moved to Washington, DC, in 1974. Suzan was the news director for the American Indian Press Association. She also served as the director of communications for the National Congress of American Indians.

Suzan continues to work for Native rights. She has pushed for better laws about how museums handle Native artifacts and human remains. She has worked in the federal government. She has argued that Native people deserve religious freedom. She has supported Native cultural rights and helped Native nations recover more than one million acres of land. She received the Presidential Medal of Freedom in 2014, which is the highest honor the United States can give someone who didn't also serve in the military.

"You don't dance in the end zone just because you got close to the goal line... You dance after you score."

EXPLORE MORE!

You can learn more about Native history at the National Museum of the American Indian in Washington, DC.

✳ ELOUISE COBELL ✳

(1945–2011)

Elouise Cobell was a Blackfeet elder, activist, and banker. She fought to make sure the government kept its promises to Native nations.

Elouise was born in Montana in 1945. She was descended from Mountain Chief, who was a renowned Blackfeet leader. Elouise's Blackfeet name means "Yellow Bird Woman."

Elouise had grown up hearing about what was known as the Starvation Winter of 1883–1884. More than 500 Blackfeet people had died because the government had not followed through on its promises. She knew that **Indian agents** on the reservation often refused to help Blackfeet people in need. She didn't understand why the Blackfeet were treated that way.

Elouise became the treasurer of the Blackfeet Nation after she finished an accounting program. She realized the numbers weren't adding up. Companies were taking oil off the reservation, but the Blackfeet weren't getting paid for it—and nobody would tell her why. She learned that Native nations across the country were being treated the same way.

In 1996, she filed a lawsuit against the Department of the Interior. The lawsuit claimed that the department had purposely mismanaged the funds it held for Native people. It would take decades for the case to be resolved. It was finally settled in

2009 for $3.4 billion. Some of the money would go to the people in the lawsuit, while some of it would help buy back Native lands.

Elouise died from cancer in 2011, just months after the settlement was finalized. The Native people in the lawsuit started receiving their first checks in December of 2012. Many people used these funds to heat their homes, buy food, or go to the doctor. Others donated their money to others in honor of Elouise. She may not have lived to see the ultimate results of her efforts, but Elouise helped change the lives of thousands of Native people.

"I know I am doing the right thing."

EXPLORE MORE!

Learning about tragedies like the Starvation Winter pushed Elouise to fight for justice for Native people.

WILMA MANKILLER

(1945–2010)

Wilma Mankiller was a Cherokee leader. She was the first woman elected to be the **principal chief** of the Cherokee Nation.

Wilma was born on the Cherokee Nation reservation in Oklahoma in 1945. She was the sixth of eleven children. Wilma, her parents, and her siblings worked together to provide for the family.

The U.S. Congress passed what's known as the **Indian Relocation Act** in 1956. The government wanted to encourage Native people to leave their reservations for bigger cities. The government promised Native people that they'd have good jobs and good places to live, but that wasn't always the case.

Wilma's family moved to the San Francisco Bay Area, in California. The government's promises turned out to be lies. It wasn't easy for her parents to find good jobs. They didn't have access to good housing for their family. As an adult, Wilma was inspired by the Native rights activists who held protests in the Bay Area and across the country. She moved her daughters back to Oklahoma. She wanted to be closer to her community.

Wilma started working for the tribal government and helped raise money for programs on the reservation. Soon she was asked to do more and more to help people on the reservation. The principal chief asked her to run as his deputy chief in 1983. They won the election. Wilma was the first woman to serve as deputy chief. Then she was elected principal chief in 1987. It was the first time the Cherokee had chosen a woman to serve as their principal chief.

Wilma served as principal chief until 1995. She was a groundbreaking leader. Throughout her life, she was recognized for the many ways she helped support Cherokee people and the Cherokee Nation. She received many awards throughout her lifetime, including the Presidential Medal of Freedom. She died in 2010 and is still honored for her advocacy work.

“I want to be remembered as the person who helped us restore faith in ourselves.”

EXPLORE MORE!

To learn more about Cherokee history, visit the Cherokee National History Museum in Tahlequah, Oklahoma.

FAITH SPOTTED EAGLE

(1948–)

Faith Spotted Eagle is an activist and a politician. She was the first Native woman to win an Electoral College vote during a presidential election. Even though she hadn't run for office, a member of the Electoral College cast a vote for her during the 2016 election.

Faith is Ihanktonwan, or Yankton Dakota. She was born in the village of White Swan in North Dakota in 1948. But Faith can never go back to the place she was born. White Swan was flooded in the 1950s after the creation of the Fort Randall Dam, which was built by the U.S. Army Corps of Engineers to help control flooding, generate electricity, and provide water. When Faith was a little girl, her father took her fishing at the lake created by the dam. He told her that one day she'd have to do something about the destruction caused by the dam.

Faith's father was right. She's spent her life advocating for Native rights, Native ceremonies, and the environment. She helped create the Brave Heart Society, which is a group of women on the Yankton Reservation who help restore cultural practices, including a ceremony called Isnati Awica Dowanpi.

It's a coming-of-age ceremony for young women. Faith also teaches the Dakota language to help keep it alive.

Faith advocates for the environment. She has protested against the Keystone XL (KXL) Pipeline and the Dakota Access Pipeline (DAPL). These pipelines carry crude oil from oil fields to refineries where it's made into products such as gasoline and diesel. Many Native people have protested the construction of pipelines such as the KXL and the DAPL. Some of these pipelines are built near Native cemeteries, sacred sites, or important water sources.

In 2016, Faith received an electoral vote in the presidential election—but she wasn't even running for president! An elector in Washington state wrote Faith's name in, making her the first Native American to receive an electoral vote for president.

Faith Spotted Eagle has dedicated her life to causes she cares about. She fights for the environment. She leads cultural ceremonies. She teaches young Native people to be proud of who they are and where they come from.

"The battle that we're fighting is 500 years old… The resistance has always been in my blood and my spirit since I was born."

EXPLORE MORE!

Check out *Native Americans in History: A History Book for Kids* to learn more about Native people who've made a difference.

MINNIE TWO SHOES

(1950–2010)

Minnie Two Shoes was a citizen of the Fort Peck Assiniboine and Sioux Tribes. She was a teacher, journalist, and activist. She also helped create the Native American Journalists Association.

Minnie was born on the Fort Peck Reservation in Montana in 1950. She had five sisters and one brother. She was famous for having a great sense of humor. This sense of humor would find its way into her writing throughout her career, and it would help teach people about Native rights issues and Native activism.

In 1970, Minnie's first journalism job was as a publicist for the American Indian Movement. Known as AIM, the organization had been founded in Minneapolis, Minnesota, in 1968 as a response to police brutality against Native people. AIM wanted people across the country to learn more about the issues Native people faced. As a publicist, Minnie helped bring attention to AIM's cause.

In the 1980s, Minnie started writing for a women-run newspaper called *Wotanin Wowapi*. Her column was called "Red Road Home." While the columns were filled with her trademark humor, she also wasn't afraid to speak out against injustice. In 1983, Minnie was among a group of Native journalists who came together to create the Native American Press Association. The group changed its name to the Native American Journalists Association (NAJA) in 1990, and today it's known as the Indigenous Journalists Association. The organization helps encourage Native journalists and supports accurate portrayals of Native people in journalism.

Minnie eventually moved to Minneapolis. She spent the rest of her life as a writer and as a mentor to young Native journalists. She helped NAJA grow from 30 members to almost 500. She died in 2010 at the age of 60. She was a lifelong advocate for Native people and Native issues, and she is remembered as an activist and a mentor.

“[As] journalists we [are] very special people, and we have a very serious responsibility, but that doesn’t mean we can’t have fun along the way!”

EXPLORE MORE!

In 2024, the Indigenous Journalists Association announced the creation of the Minnie Two Shoes Award for Excellence in Tribal Media. It honors people who work at a local newspaper, radio or TV station, or digital outlet that centers a tribal nation.

KATSI COOK

(1952–)

Katsi Cook is a Mohawk midwife, environmentalist, activist, and advocate.

Known as Katsi (pronounced Gudji), Sherrill Elizabeth Tekatsitsiakawa Cook was born in 1952. She was born on the lands of the Mohawk Nation at Akwesasne, which stretches across parts of the United States and Canada. She was the youngest of four children. Her grandmother was a midwife who delivered Katsi and many other babies on the reservation. Katsi's father had been a pilot in World War II and the Korean War, and he died in a plane crash when she was a baby. Her mother also died when Katsi was young, and Katsi went to live with her grandmother.

While Katsi went to Catholic boarding schools, she also learned traditional cultural practices. She was one of the first class of women accepted at Dartmouth College, but she left college in the early 1970s to join the American Indian Movement (AIM). AIM was part of a growing number of organizations and movements that were fighting for Native rights.

Katsi decided to become a midwife in 1977. She had gone to a conference that talked about what it meant for Native people to protect their **sovereignty** and their rights. For people like

Katsi, this included helping Native women give birth like their ancestors did. The process could involve special ceremonies, foods, or rituals. And her advocacy work didn't end once babies were born. In the 1980s, she started researching how environmental issues affect ways of life for Native people.

Today, Katsi continues to advocate for Native rights and the environment. Native nations such as the Mohawk often struggle with the effects of climate change and pollution. Because of that, Katsi builds networks to support women and women's health issues. She develops training programs for Native midwives. Katsi has also created several organizations that support Mohawk people on the reservation, and she works to make sure that Mohawk people—and Indigenous people around the world—can practice their traditions and live in safe environments.

> “The story of where I come from begins with my mother.”

EXPLORE MORE!

The Mohawk are one of the original five nations of the Haudenosaunee Confederacy. The Mohawk came together with the Oneida, Onondaga, Cayuga, and Seneca to create a peaceful way of making decisions together. Today, the Confederacy also includes the Tuscarora.

BONNIE RED ELK

(1952–2015)

Bonnie Red Elk was a citizen of the Fort Peck Assiniboine and Sioux Tribes. She was a journalist and a newspaper editor.

Bonnie was born in Poplar, Montana, in 1952. Her Native name, A Stupi Win, means "Good Star Woman." Her ancestor, John Lone Dog, had been the last chief on the reservation. He had kept what is called a "buffalo robe winter count," which is a way of keeping a record of important events through pictographs, which are images drawn to depict words or phrases. Robes like this could be considered early versions of Native newspapers. Like her ancestors, Bonnie knew that it was important for Native people to keep records of what was happening in their world.

Bonnie didn't have any experience as a journalist, but she started working as a reporter at the tribal newspaper, *Wotanin Wowapi*, in 1975. A year later, she became the editor. While Bonnie wrote about many aspects of life on the reservation, she mostly covered the tribal government. This helped people on the reservation know what was happening. Like Minnie Two Shoes, Bonnie was also a founding member of what's now known as the Indigenous Journalists Association.

In 2006, Bonnie discovered that the tribal chairman was using tribal funds for his own vacations. She knew she was risking her job as the editor of the tribe's official newspaper by researching the story. The chairman fired her from the job she'd had for 30 years. But Bonnie didn't give up. Instead, she and her sister started their own newspaper, the *Fort Peck Journal*.

It was a huge risk. They started the newspaper with equipment that they borrowed or that people donated. And it paid off. Bonnie's decision to start her own newspaper earned her the support of many people on the reservation. She was celebrated for her courage, and she earned several awards for her work. The readership for the *Fort Peck Journal* grew larger and larger. People on the reservation knew that they could trust Bonnie and her writing. Bonnie died in 2015 after suffering a stroke the year before.

Bonnie wasn't a fan of speaking in public—she preferred to express herself through her writing. After she passed, the president of NAJA praised Bonnie, saying, "She just did what she felt was right and she stuck to it."

EXPLORE MORE!

The *Fort Peck Journal* is still published today!

PATTI CATALANO

(1953–)

Patti Catalano is a Mi'kmaw runner. In 1980, she became the fastest American woman to run a marathon!

Patti was born in 1953, and she grew up in Massachusetts. She was the oldest of nine children. Her mother was Mi'kmaw, and her father was Irish. Like many other Native people, Patti's mother had dealt with years of racism and discrimination because she was Native. She didn't want her children to be targeted the way she had been, so she tried to hide the fact that she and her children were Native. When Patti was a teenager, her mother cut off her long hair so she couldn't wear it in braids.

Patti started running in 1976 when she was 23. She wasn't happy with her life, and she needed to find a healthy solution. Once she ran for the first time, she knew she had found what could make her happy. She won the very first race she entered, and a few months later she ran—and won—her first marathon, which is 26.2 miles!

In 1980, she was one of the first women to sign a contract as a professional runner. She kept winning races, but it wasn't enough for Patti. She wanted to be the first American woman to run a marathon in under two and a half hours. She had already set the world record, but it wasn't fast enough. In November of 1980, she ran the New York City Marathon in 2 hours and 29 minutes. She had finally done what she'd set out to do!

By the end of her career, Patti had set American and world records in the 5-mile, 10-mile, 10K, 15K, 20K, 30K, and half-marathon distances. She had won the Honolulu Marathon four times, and she'd finished second at the famous Boston Marathon three times. Running had taken her around the world, and it had changed her life. Patti continues to run, and she also mentors and motivates the next generation of Native runners.

“We are resilient. We always get back up, and we are still here.”

EXPLORE MORE!

Women were not allowed to enter the Boston Marathon until 1972.

ROBIN WALL KIMMERER

(1953–)

Robin Wall Kimmerer is a Citizen Potawatomi botanist and author. Her book *Braiding Sweetgrass* has won many bestseller awards.

Robin was born in New York in 1953. As a kid, she loved spending time outside. Her parents always encouraged her, and it would help shape her future career. Her grandfather had been sent to the Carlisle Indian Industrial School, and Robin knew that these boarding schools had been designed to destroy Native cultures and languages. She also knew that it's important for Native people to learn and teach their ways of life.

Robin earned her bachelor's and master's degrees in botany, which is the scientific study of plants. She earned her PhD in plant ecology, then became a college professor. Robin's work includes a focus on what's called TEK, or Traditional Ecological Knowledge. TEK centers Native and Indigenous practices and beliefs about the relationships living things have with each other and their environment.

Western scientific practices have usually ignored Native beliefs. But scholars like Robin are trying to change that.

They combine their scientific training with Native systems of knowledge. This gives them a better understanding of the world around them. They learn about things like controlled burning and how to protect important crops like wild rice. They learn the best ways to take care of our plant and animal relatives.

Today, Robin continues to conduct research, teach college classes, and write books. She works with Native nations to help restore plants that are important to Native people. She wants to make these areas of study easier for Native students to access. She helps other scientists learn about TEK, and she helps them learn how to do their research in a way that respects Native knowledge and cultural practices.

“Whatever our gift, we are called to give it and to dance for the renewal of the world.”

EXPLORE MORE!

To learn more about Robin's work, check out *Braiding Sweetgrass for Young Adults*.

LOUISE ERDRICH

(1954–)

Louise Erdrich is an award-winning writer. Many of her books are inspired by traditional stories or historical events.

Louise was born in Little Falls, Minnesota, and grew up in Wahpeton, North Dakota. Her father was German American, and her mother was a citizen of the Turtle Mountain Band of Chippewa Indians. Louise is the oldest of seven children. Her parents were teachers, and she and her siblings spent a lot of time reading and learning. Louise loved to write. Her parents were her biggest cheerleaders. Her dad gave her a nickel for every story she wrote, and her mother made covers for her books.

Louise entered Dartmouth College in 1972. She was one of the first women admitted to the college, where she decided to major in English. She had grown up around storytellers, and she realized she could use her family's history and stories in her writing. Louise earned a master's degree, then returned to Dartmouth as a writer-in-residence. This means she was able to dedicate more time to writing. Louise published her first book in 1984. It was called *Love Medicine*. It won the National Book Critics Circle Award, which is one of the most prestigious book awards.

Louise is best known as a writer for adults, but she has also written children's books, including the Birchbark series, which covers 100 years in the life of an Ojibwe family. She has also written books of poetry. Many of her books are fictional, but others are based on historical events. *The Round House*, published in 2012, won the National Book Award for Fiction. *The Night Watchman*, published in 2020, won the Pulitzer Prize for Fiction.

Today, Louise continues to write. She stays inspired by thinking about her ancestors and their experiences. She also helps support other authors. She owns a bookstore in Minneapolis called Birchbark Books. She and her sister, Heid, also have a publishing company called Wiigwaas Press. They only publish books that are written in Ojibwe. *Wiigwaas* means "birchbark" in Ojibwe.

"I grew up knowing who I was and accepting all parts of myself. And this is a part that I realized would not have existed had my grandfather not fought for it."

EXPLORE MORE!

Want to read some of Louise's books? Check out *The Birchbark House*, *The Game of Silence*, *The Porcupine Year*, *Chickadee*, and *Makoons*.

LORELEI DeCORA MEANS

(1954–)

Lorelei DeCora Means is a Winnebago (Ho-Chunk) nurse, activist, and organizer.

Lorelei was born on the Winnebago Reservation in Nebraska in 1954. Her mother was Lakota, but Lorelei grew up among her Ho-Chunk relatives in Nebraska. She started fighting for Native rights when she was just a teenager. There was a book in her high school library that used racist depictions of Native people. She and her family pushed the school district to remove the book from the library.

In 1973, members of the American Indian Movement responded to a call for help from people at the Pine Ridge Reservation in South Dakota. Alongside the people of Pine Ridge, AIM's protest called attention to unsafe conditions on the reservation. Lorelei was only 19, but she helped set up a clinic for the protesters when they needed medical care. She organized medical supplies. She helped coordinate teams of doctors and nurses, and she trained other protesters in basic medical care.

Lorelei's dedication to Native issues didn't end after the occupation. In 1978, Lorelei—along with other Native women, including Janet McCloud and Madonna Thunder Hawk—founded an organization called Women of All Red Nations (WARN). The Native women of WARN worked to protect Native lands and waters, and they called for the protection of Native women.

Lorelei knew that access to health care was important for Native people. She earned a degree in nursing in the 1980s and helped set up the Porcupine Clinic in South Dakota. It was the first community-owned and operated clinic on a reservation, and it offers important care for people in the region. Many Native people struggle with health issues such as diabetes, and Lorelei advocates for better treatment and prevention.

“In my life, what’s driven me in the work that I do has always been the spiritual side.”

EXPLORE MORE!

In addition to their work in Minneapolis, AIM organized national protests such as the Trail of Broken Treaties in 1972 and the Longest Walk in 1978.

✳ LaDONNA BRAVE BULL ALLARD ✳

(1956–2021)

LaDonna Brave Bull Allard was a Dakota and Lakota historian, genealogist, and leader of the water protector movement, which pushed back against the construction of oil pipelines on tribal or sacred lands.

LaDonna was born in North Dakota in 1956. She was known as Tamaka Waste Win, or "Good Earth Woman." As a child, she spent a lot of time with her grandmothers. She would bring her family drinking water from the Cannonball River. She learned that the U.S. government had destroyed a sacred site along the river. After college, she worked for the Standing Rock Sioux Tribe in North Dakota as the tribal historian and genealogist. This meant that she helped protect the tribe's cultural heritage and researched its history and family connections. She also helped the tribe open an office of historic preservation and a tourism office.

In the 2010s, LaDonna learned about a new pipeline. It was called the Dakota Access Pipeline. It would carry oil from North Dakota to Illinois, and it would cut very close to the Standing Rock Reservation. The construction of the pipeline would break a treaty the government had made with Native nations in 1868. It could damage important water supplies and disrupt sacred sites—including the grave of one of LaDonna's sons. Native people started organizing protests against the pipeline. LaDonna set up a camp for the protesters on her land. She called it Sacred Stone Camp.

People came to the protest camps from all over the world. They prayed and held ceremonies. Younger Native people organized a relay run from Standing Rock to Washington, DC. The water protector movement brought together people from many different Native nations. The governor of North Dakota ordered that the protest camps be closed in 2017, but LaDonna and the other water protectors never gave up.

LaDonna never saw herself as an activist. She never thought of herself as a protester. But she knew what she had to do to protect Native lands, water sources, and sacred sites. LaDonna had helped inspire a global movement in support of tribal sovereignty by bringing international attention to the issues Native people faced. Thanks to people like LaDonna, the water protectors called on the government to uphold the treaties it had made with Native nations.

> "We want to determine our own future."

EXPLORE MORE!

Sacred Stone Camp was one of several major protest camps that rose against the Dakota Access Pipeline.

LORI ARVISO ALVORD

(1958–)

Lori Arviso Alvord is a Diné (Navajo) surgeon and author. She is the first Diné woman to have become a board-certified surgeon.

Lori was born in 1958 in a military hospital in Washington state. Her father was Diné, and her mother's ancestors came from Europe. After Lori was born, her family moved to the reservation. Today, the Navajo Nation's lands are located in northeastern Arizona, northwestern New Mexico, and southeastern Utah. Lori often felt like she was part of two different worlds. As a child, she didn't know doctors who were Diné—or women. Neither of her parents had gone to college, but they always encouraged Lori and her two younger sisters to get an education and follow their dreams.

Lori was only 16 years old when she graduated from high school. She was accepted to Dartmouth College in New Hampshire. She had never been that far away from home before. She missed her family and the familiar foods. She found friends in other Native students who had come to Dartmouth from across the country.

After college, she worked for a medical researcher. He encouraged her to go to medical school. Lori didn't know if she could do it, but she started taking premed classes at the University of New Mexico before applying to medical school. She fell in love with surgery, but she knew it was a competitive field—and that very few surgeons were women. But she kept studying and practicing, and she made it into the surgical training program.

Lori went back to the reservation to practice medicine after she finished her training. She knew that Diné people were not always comfortable around non-Native doctors. Diné traditions did not follow the same steps that most doctors did. So Lori found ways to incorporate Diné traditions into her practice. She would introduce herself in Navajo to make people more comfortable. Traditional Diné practitioners would perform ceremonies for the patients at the hospital. Her patients learned that they could trust her, and their surgeries seemed to be much more successful. Lori's decisions helped save lives, and she continues to show other doctors how they can work with Native patients.

> "Everything in life is connected."

EXPLORE MORE!

The traditional Diné belief of "walking in beauty" teaches Diné people to live a balanced and harmonious life.

* RYNELDI BECENTI *

(1971–)

Ryneldi Becenti is a retired Diné (Navajo) basketball player. She was the first Native woman to play in the Women's National Basketball Association (WNBA).

Ryneldi was born in 1971 and grew up on the Navajo Nation. She was one of five children—and the only girl. Her father loved basketball, and Ryneldi loved watching basketball games with him. She also loved watching her parents play basketball. Her family had a dirt court, and Ryneldi spent hours outside practicing her shooting and ball handling. She played basketball at Window Rock High School, and she helped her team win a state championship in 1988.

Ryneldi started her college basketball career at Scottsdale Community College (SCC) in Arizona. As a point guard, she averaged 21 points per game as a sophomore. She led her team to 44 wins over two seasons. Then she transferred to Arizona State University (ASU). With Ryneldi as their point guard, ASU made it to the NCAA Tournament for the first time in nine years. People from the Navajo Nation loved watching her play, and there was always a huge turnout for her home games.

After college, Ryneldi played for the U.S. team at the World University Games in New York. She played basketball in Sweden and Greece before receiving an invitation to try out for a new women's professional basketball organization in the United States. She signed with the Phoenix Mercury, making her the first Native woman to play in the WNBA.

Ryneldi retired after one season because her father was sick and she needed to take care of him. But her legacy lives on. Both SCC and ASU retired her jersey, and she was the first women's basketball player to have her jersey retired at ASU. No other women's basketball player at either school will ever wear #21 again. After she stopped playing professionally, Ryneldi started coaching young Native basketball players. She wants to make sure Native players can have the same opportunities as other athletes.

"My stories make me stronger."

EXPLORE MORE!

Ryneldi once appeared on an episode of *Sesame Street*.

ELIZABETH JAMES-PERRY

(1973–)

Elizabeth James-Perry is a Aquinnah Wampanoag artist, educator, and lecturer.

Elizabeth was born in 1973. She is a citizen of the Wampanoag Tribe of Gay Head (Aquinnah) in Massachusetts. Her mother, Patricia, was also an artist. Patricia's work focused on scrimshaw, which means she made engravings, scrollwork, and carvings on bone or ivory. If Elizabeth sat still, Patricia would let her watch while Patricia worked. She allowed Elizabeth to touch the materials and would explain what she was doing.

Elizabeth grew up around artists and educators. She learned traditional Wampanoag songs from her cousin Tony, and her cousin Helen taught her how to weave traditional baskets. Other artists taught her how to make coiled pottery and porcupine quillwork. Her brother Jonathan is also an artist and performer.

Elizabeth earned a degree in marine science at the University of Massachusetts Dartmouth. Her marine science education and her art background often work together. She helps restore and reintroduce native plants on Wampanoag lands, and she works with colleges and conservation agencies to bring back native plant species. She also uses many natural materials like quahog – a type of edible clam that's found on the Atlantic coast – and milkweed in her work. She knows that these materials are important to Wampanoag people, culture, and history.

Elizabeth makes hand-sculpted beads, creates natural dyes from local plants, and spins plant fibers to use as she weaves baskets. She also uses her artwork to teach people about Wampanoag art and history. Wampum, for instance, are shell beads that were used in ceremonies and as currency, and they play an important part in Elizabeth's art. As a Native artist, Elizabeth's work is tied to both Wampanoag history and the natural world.

“Art is one’s soul speaking to another, expressing our humanity and humor.”

EXPLORE MORE!

The ancestors of the Wampanoag have lived at Aquinnah (Gay Head), on what’s now the island of Martha’s Vineyard, for more than 10,000 years.

NICOLE AUNAPU MANN

(1977–)

Nicole Aunapu Mann is a **test pilot** and NASA astronaut. In 2022, she became the first Native woman to go to space.

A citizen of the Wailacki of the Round Valley Indian Tribes, Nicole was born in Petaluma, California, in 1977. She grew up in Sonoma County, which is about two hours away from the Round Valley Reservation. As a kid, Nicole always loved math and science. She also played soccer. Her determination as both an athlete and a student helped her find her path in life.

Nicole studied engineering at the U.S. Naval Academy and also joined the soccer team. She trained as a test pilot in the U.S. Marine Corps and flew 47 **combat missions** in Iraq and Afghanistan. She was one of the first women to fly in combat for the Marines. She earned a master's degree in mechanical engineering, but she didn't know what she wanted to do next. Then she started reading about NASA astronauts. She was one of only eight people chosen as an astronaut candidate in 2013.

Nicole went to space in 2022, serving as the commander of a four-person crew. She took two spacewalks, which is when an astronaut leaves the space station or spacecraft to work outside the vehicle. On her spacewalks, she upgraded the solar panels that helped power the International Space Station (ISS). She also performed many scientific experiments during her 157-day mission to space. Inside the ISS, she tested ways to grow vegetables and how to 3D-print different materials.

Back on Earth, Nicole has inspired future generations of hopeful astronauts. She gives talks about her experiences. She wants kids to see what it's like to be an astronaut and break barriers. Even though she's already been to space, Nicole is still looking ahead. She's training for future missions as part of a NASA program that wants to send a woman to the moon.

"It makes you reflect on where we all came from and how we are all living on this planet."

EXPLORE MORE!

Nicole's mother had hung a dream catcher in Nicole's childhood bedroom, and Nicole took that dream catcher with her to space in 2022.

LORI PIESTEWA

(1979–2003)

Lori Piestewa was an army soldier. She was the first Native woman to die in combat while serving in the U.S. military. She was also the first female American soldier to die in the Iraq War.

Lori was born in Tuba City, Arizona, in 1979. Her father is Hopi, and her mother is Mexican American. Her grandfather had served in World War II, and her father served in the Vietnam War. They were very proud of their military service. Lori's Hopi name translates to "White Bear Girl." In high school, she pitched and played second base on her school's softball team. She also participated in the Reserve Officers' Training Corps (ROTC).

Lori joined the military in 2001, just a few years after she graduated from high school. She served as a member of the U.S. Army's 507th Maintenance Company in Iraq. In 2003, her unit accidentally made a wrong turn and drove into an ambush. Lori was driving one of the vehicles. She tried to get herself and her comrades away from the fighting. Lori was severely wounded during the ambush, and she died from her injuries in an Iraqi hospital.

After her death, Lori was awarded the Purple Heart. The Purple Heart is given to soldiers who have been wounded or killed while serving in the U.S. military. She was also awarded the Prisoner of War Medal. The U.S. Army promoted her from private first class to specialist.

Lori's friends and family still work to keep her memory alive. There are now a number of memorials that celebrate Lori. In 2008, a peak in the Phoenix Mountains was officially renamed Piestewa Peak. The Lori Piestewa National Native American Games have brought athletes together from across the country since 2003. Native people from all over the United States continue to honor Lori's sacrifice.

Lori's son, Brandon Piestewa, once said, "My mother's example has inspired many women who have followed in her footsteps, serving their country with the same courage and determination that she embodied."

EXPLORE MORE!

Want to learn more about how Native people have participated in the U.S. military? Check out the documentary called *The Warrior Tradition*.

LILY GLADSTONE

(1986–)

Lily Gladstone is a Blackfeet and Nez Perce actor. Lily was the first Native person to win a Golden Globe for Best Actress and the first Native person nominated for an Academy Award for Best Actress.

Lily was born in Kalispell, Montana, in 1986, and grew up on the Blackfeet Indian Reservation in northwestern Montana. It didn't take long for Lily to choose a career: after watching *Return of the Jedi* at 5 years old, Lily decided to be an Ewok! Lily started acting in plays and musicals, and in their high school yearbook their classmates voted them "most likely to win an Oscar."

Lily studied acting and directing at the University of Montana. Lily made their film debut in 2012 and started landing bigger roles in 2016. Lily acted in film and on stage and hosted an educational series before landing the biggest role in their career in 2023.

Lily starred in a film called *Killers of the Flower Moon*. The movie was based on true events in Osage history, and Lily's performance in the film also made history. In 2024, Lily became the first Native person to win a Golden Globe for Best Actress. A few weeks later, Lily was the first Native woman to be nominated for an Academy Award for Best Actress. While Lily didn't win the Oscar, Lily's performance in the movie brought attention to some of the issues that Native nations had faced in the past.

Lily continues to act in movies and television shows. Lily also advocates for Native actors, Native people, and Native communities. They hope that movie studios will move past stereotypical depictions of Native people. They call attention to the struggles that Native women face. In March of 2024, the Blackfeet Nation hosted Lily Gladstone Day. Elementary school children on the reservation made a book for Lily. Community members honored Lily with a ceremony and a feast.

“I wouldn’t have been able to do anything good with my life if I didn’t come from good people.”

EXPLORE MORE!

Lily was also the first Native actor to win the Screen Actors Guild Award for Outstanding Performance by a Female Actor in a Leading Role, again for their performance in *Killers of the Flower Moon*.

JOCELYNE LAROCQUE

(1988–)

Jocelyne Larocque is a Métis professional hockey player. She became the first Indigenous woman to play hockey in the Winter Olympics when she played at the 2014 games in Sochi, Russia.

Jocelyne was born in the small town of Ste. Anne, Manitoba, Canada, in 1988. There weren't any girls' hockey teams around, so Jocelyne grew up playing on boys' teams. She was the first girl to play in the Winnipeg High School Hockey League. She played college hockey at the University of Minnesota Duluth. The Bulldogs won the national tournament in 2008 and 2010 with Jocelyne on the line.

Jocelyne played her first game on Canada's national team in 2008. She didn't make the cut for the 2010 Olympic team, but she made her first Olympic appearance in 2014. As a defensive player, she helped Canada win its fourth straight gold medal in women's hockey.

There weren't many opportunities for women to play professional hockey in the United States and Canada, and the few small leagues couldn't pay their players very much.

That changed in 2024 with the creation of the Professional Women's Hockey League (PWHL). The PWHL started with six teams—three in the United States, and three in Canada. Jocelyne was the second player chosen for a team. She was drafted by the Toronto Sceptres and played in the first-ever PWHL game, held on January 2, 2024. She was traded to the Ottawa Charge in 2025.

Jocelyne continues to make history. In 2025, she became the first Canadian defender—and only the fifth player in history—to play in 200 games for Team Canada's women's hockey team. As of 2025, she has played in three Olympic Games, winning two gold medals and one silver medal. Jocelyne's perseverance has inspired many girls and Indigenous kids who want to play hockey.

> “My dad is Métis and he made sure I knew where I came from.”

EXPLORE MORE!

Ste. Anne may be a small town, but Jocelyne was one of three Ste. Anne hockey players in the 2008–2009 women's "Frozen Four," the name given to the teams competing in the Division I and II semifinal and championship games. The other two players were Melanie Gagnon (University of Minnesota) and Bailey Bram (Mercyhurst University).

MICHAELA GOADE

(c. 1990–)

Michaela Goade is a Tlingit and Haida illustrator. She has illustrated many award-winning children's books.

Michaela was born in Juneau, Alaska. She is Tlingit and Haida. The Tlingit and Haida are Indigenous nations from the Pacific Northwest, and they are both known for their beautiful art. Michaela grew up picking berries with her mother and her sister, and she would also go out fishing with her family. The many different landscapes in Alaska—from the temperate rainforest to the glaciers and the mountains—would later inspire Michaela's art.

Michaela's family always supported her dreams of being an artist. She earned a degree in graphic design and marketing from Fort Lewis College in Colorado. She worked as an art director in Anchorage, Alaska, for two years before she moved back to Juneau to illustrate a series of books for the Tlingit tribe. The first was called *Shanyaak'utlaax̱: Salmon Boy*. It was based on a traditional Tlingit story about a boy who offended the Salmon People by throwing away an old piece of fish. The book was printed in both Tlingit and English.

In 2021, Michaela made history when she won the Caldecott Medal for her watercolor illustrations in *We Are Water Protectors*. The book, written by Native author Carole Lindstrom, tells the story of an Ojibwe girl who fights against an oil pipeline to protect her peoples' water source. Michaela was the first Indigenous artist—and the first woman of color—to win the highest award for children's book illustration.

Michaela continues to inspire people with her artwork. She illustrated a Google Doodle featuring Tlingit activist Elizabeth Peratrovich, and she created a picture book adaptation of a Joy Harjo poem. Her artwork demonstrates the many different elements of Native histories, and it offers Native and non-Native readers a chance to explore the beauty of Native cultures. She also mentors younger illustrators. She hopes that her work can help showcase the diversity of Native experiences.

“When we care about these lands, this planet, that’s when change happens. When we care, we protect.”

EXPLORE MORE!

We Are Water Protectors was inspired by the protests against the Dakota Access Pipeline.

MARY KILLMAN

(1991–)

Mary Killman is a Citizen Potawatomi synchronized swimmer.

Mary was born in Ada, Oklahoma, in 1991, and grew up in McKinney, Texas. Mary started swimming when she was very young, competing in her first race when she was only 5 years old. At age 11, she started doing synchronized swimming, which is when a team of swimmers performs a choreographed routine to music. Mary gave up racing when she was 15 to focus on synchronized swimming. Mary's dedication helped her earn a spot on her first national team.

Mary competed in the 2009 U.S. National Championships, and she finished third in the solo competition, second in the duet competition, and first in the team competition. Synchronized swimming is a very challenging sport. After she and her partner, Mariya Koroleva, started swimming together in August of 2011, they practiced up to twelve hours a day, six days a week.

A few months later, they won a silver medal at the Pan American Games in Mexico. They were chosen to represent the United States in the 2012 London Olympics, and they placed seventh at the Olympic qualifiers. Since the United States didn't qualify for the team event, Mary and Mariya were the only American synchronized swimmers to compete in the London games.

After the Olympics, Mary went to college at Lindenwood University. She joined their synchronized swimming team. Even though she was a busy college student, she was still able to win a silver medal at the 2015 Pan American Games in Toronto. She earned 36 medals during her 15-year career, and she was inducted into the USA Artistic Swimming Athlete Hall of Fame in 2021. She has always been proud of her heritage, and some of her earliest routines were set to Native music.

> "The easier it looks, the better you are at it."

EXPLORE MORE!

Synchronized swimmers are not allowed to touch the bottom of the pool during their routines. Underwater cameras and referees are used to make sure everyone follows the rules.

JANEE' KASSANAVOID

(1995–)

Janee' Kassanavoid is a Comanche track and field athlete. She specializes in the hammer throw, in which an athlete uses both hands to see how far they can throw a metal ball.

Janee' was born in Lawson, Missouri, in 1995. Her father was diagnosed with cancer when she was only 8 years old, and Janee' was devastated when he died. He had been her biggest cheerleader and her strongest connection to her Comanche culture. He wanted his kids to have a better life than he'd had in Oklahoma, and he saw sports as their best option.

Janee' played multiple sports when she was growing up as a way to honor her dad. She lettered in softball, volleyball, basketball, and track and field in high school. Her dad's health issues inspired her to go to college so she could improve health care among Native people. She went to college at Kansas State University, where she set track and field records in the weight throw and the hammer throw.

Janee' wanted to be a professional athlete, but it wasn't always easy. She didn't see many women who looked like her competing in track and field. She missed the qualifying mark for the 2021 Olympic team by five centimeters—less than two inches. But Janee' didn't give up. In 2022, she became the first Native woman to win a medal at the World Athletics Championships.

Janee's bronze medal inspired her to keep pushing herself. Through her journey as a professional athlete, Janee' wants to inspire others, bring people together, and make a difference for future generations. She wants to teach others about Native histories and Native cultures. She wants to remind the world that Native people have always been here, and that they will always be here.

"From an early age, I came to understand that my people are warriors."

EXPLORE MORE!

As of 2025, Janee's personal best hammer throw was 78 meters—or 255 feet and almost 11 inches!

✳ ABBY ROQUE ✳

(1997–)

Abby Roque is a professional hockey player. She was the first Indigenous player named to the USA Women's Hockey Team.

Abby was born in Sault Ste. Marie, Michigan, in 1997. She is Ojibwe of the Wahnapitae First Nation, an Indigenous nation based in Ontario, Canada. Abby grew up surrounded by her culture. She'd go to **powwows** at the ice rink, and school assemblies always started with drum circles. She and her sister learned to figure skate on a rink in their backyard, and her aunt gave her hockey skates for Christmas a few years later.

There weren't many hockey teams for girls, so Abby played with the boys. She played hockey at the University of Wisconsin after she graduated from high school, and she became one of the best women's hockey players in the university's history. But she still faced challenges along the way.

She had been one of many Indigenous people in her hometown, but that changed when she went to college. She had to find ways to stay connected to her culture, so she started doing research and reading more books. Her career was also disrupted by the COVID-19 pandemic. She was finally able to join the U.S. women's national team in 2022 for the Beijing Winter Olympics, and the Americans brought home the silver medal.

Abby joined the New York Sirens professional women's hockey team in 2023. Indigenous people across the country love to watch her play. Abby knows that she's a role model for Indigenous kids, especially because she's the first Indigenous woman to play for the national team. Hockey is an expensive sport, and Abby works to make hockey more affordable for kids like her. She wants to make sure all kids have a chance to play the sports they love.

“There’s definitely pressure, but it’s a great pressure to have, and it’s a responsibility I’m more than happy to do if it leads more kids to play.”

EXPLORE MORE!

In 2025, Abby scored the first “Michigan goal” in the history of the Professional Women’s Hockey League. This trick shot is very difficult, and it’s named after a goal scored by a University of Michigan men’s player in 1996.

* MADISON * HAMMOND

(1997–)

Madison Hammond is a professional soccer player. She is the first Native woman to play in the National Women's Soccer League.

Madison was born in Phoenix, Arizona. Her mother is Navajo (Diné) and San Felipe Pueblo. Madison grew up in the San Felipe Pueblo community in New Mexico. She started playing soccer when she was only 5 years old. There weren't any girls' teams, so she played on boys' teams. Her family moved to Virginia when she was 9. It wasn't always easy for Madison, but sports helped her adjust to her new life.

After high school, Madison went to college at Wake Forest University in Winston-Salem, North Carolina. She played as a defender, which means she stayed near her team's goal and tried to stop the other team from scoring. She was named team captain for her senior year. Like a lot of college athletes, Madison wanted to play professional soccer. During the COVID-19 pandemic, though, it was even harder to play professional sports.

But Madison didn't give up! She was offered a spot on a professional team in Seattle in 2020. She made her first appearance that same year. Then she joined the Angel City Football Club in 2022. She scored two goals in the 2023 season, which is very impressive for a defender. She scored her first National Women's Soccer League (NWSL) goal against her former team.

Like other athletes, Madison keeps working to improve her game. She knows she's an inspiration for other Native people. She's been an ambassador for Nike's N7 program, which encourages Native kids to participate in sports. Like Madison, all of the ambassadors are Native athletes, and together they help show Native kids that they can also pursue their dreams. In 2021, Madison got to design a Nike shoe that showcased her culture and personality.

“It takes a lot of courage to fail… But having that courage is what allows us to succeed.”

EXPLORE MORE!

Interested in soccer? See if there's an NWSL team near you at www.nwslsoccer.com.

AUTUMN PELTIER

(2004–)

Autumn Peltier is an Anishinaabe activist. She advocates for clean drinking water for Indigenous people.

Autumn was born in Wiikwemkoong Unceded Territory, Manitoulin Island, in Ontario. She grew up on the shores of Lake Huron, one of the Great Lakes. When she was 8, she went to a ceremony that inspired her future activism. She learned that many Indigenous **reserves** in Canada did not have access to clean water because of pollution and pipeline leaks. Indigenous people would have to boil the water before they could drink it, cook with it, or bathe in it.

Autumn has spent most of her life advocating for clean drinking water. In 2016, she gained international attention when she called out the Canadian prime minister, Justin Trudeau, for his policies on clean water. She was only 12 years old. She was invited to speak at the United Nations when she was 13, and she was nominated for the prestigious International Children's Peace Prize three years in a row.

Her great-aunt, Josephine Mandamin, was also known for her advocacy. As a "water walker," she walked around the Great Lakes from 2003 to 2017 to bring attention to water pollution. Josephine served as the chief water commissioner for the Anishinabek Nation for many years. This means she provided leadership and guidance on issues of water. Josephine died in 2019, and Autumn became the chief water commissioner when she was only 14.

Autumn continues to advocate for the rights of Indigenous people. In addition to her work as chief water commissioner, she advocates for environmental justice. This means that she recognizes that poor and marginalized communities are often the most affected by pollution and climate change. She brings attention to the racism that Indigenous people face. She also supports other young activists and believes that young people have the power to create change.

"I hope to see people standing up and more people taking action."

EXPLORE MORE!

As chief water commissioner, Autumn represents 39 First Nations communities in Ontario.

✳ IDLE NO MORE ✳

(2012–)

Idle No More is a protest movement that began in 2012. Its four founders are Nina Wilson, Sheelah McLean, Sylvia McAdam Saysewahum, and Jessica Gordon.

In 2012, the Canadian government proposed a new piece of legislation known as Bill C-45. Also called the Jobs and Growth Act, it would have affected Indigenous people by taking away their rights. It also would have made it harder for Indigenous nations to exercise their rights as sovereign nations.

Indigenous people also believed this bill would make it easier for governments and businesses to avoid having to prove that large projects wouldn't hurt the environment. This, in turn, could also negatively affect Indigenous communities. The first protests started in November 2012 when Nina Wilson, Sheelah McLean, Sylvia McAdam Saysewahum, and Jessica Gordon—all of whom are from Saskatchewan—started emailing each other about the bill. They posted about their concerns on Facebook, and the movement quickly grew.

People started hosting rallies and teach-ins, which are gatherings for people to learn more and raise awareness about certain issues. In December, people began holding "flash mobs" in shopping malls to bring attention to the bill and its potential consequences for Indigenous people. Most of these flash mobs included round dances, which are traditional dances that bring people together to celebrate and honor our ancestors and the land. By early 2013, supporters of Indigenous rights were holding rallies and round dances in many different countries.

Although Canada's government passed Bill C-45, the founders of Idle No More continue to support Indigenous rights in Canada and around the world. They bring attention to problems in the Canadian justice system and its often-unfair treatment of Indigenous people. They support environmental protests against pipeline development, and they support the ongoing exercise of Indigenous rights globally. They use social media to bring people together to stand up for Indigenous voices and Indigenous rights.

Sylvia McAdam Saysewahum, an Idle No More founder, has said, "It was an incredible time of prayer and just sacred gathering. It just brought so many people together."

EXPLORE MORE!

Three of the four founders of Idle No More are Indigenous. Sylvia is from the Big River First Nation, Nina is from the Kahkewistahaw First Nation, and Jessica is from the Pasqua First Nation.

MORE INSPIRING PEOPLE

BUFFALO CALF ROAD WOMAN (C. 1844–1879): Buffalo Calf Road Woman was Northern Cheyenne. She saved her brother during the Battle of the Rosebud in June of 1876, and her bravery helped rally the warriors to victory. Cheyenne people call it the Battle Where the Girl Saved Her Brother.

ELIZA "LYDA" CONLEY (1869–1946): Lyda Conley (Wyandot) was the first Native woman to work as a lawyer. She fought to protect the Wyandot burial grounds from being sold and developed.

ADA BLACKJACK (1898–1983): An Iñupiaq woman, Ada Blackjack was the sole survivor of an Arctic expedition to Wrangel Island, off the coast of Russia. After the other expedition members left or died, she lived alone on the island for eight months until she was rescued.

OFELIA ZEPEDA (1952–): Ofelia Zepeda is a Tohono O'odham poet, professor, and linguist. She wrote one of the very first O'odham grammar books.

DEB HAALAND (1960–): Deb Haaland is a Laguna Pueblo politician. She was the first Native person to serve as a Cabinet secretary. She was Secretary of the Interior from 2021 to 2025.

PEGGY FLANAGAN (1979–): Peggy Flanagan is an Ojibwe politician. She was elected lieutenant governor of Minnesota in 2018 and reelected in 2022. When she was elected, she became the highest-ranking Native woman in an elected office in the nation.

JORDAN MARIE BRINGS THREE WHITE HORSES DANIEL (1988–): Jordan is a Lakota and Diné runner and activist. She started running when she was 10 years old, and she uses running as a way to call attention to Native issues. She also helps build healthy communities through running programs for Native youth.

BRIGETTE LACQUETTE (1992–): Brigette Lacquette is a hockey player. She is from the Cote First Nation in Saskatchewan, Canada, and she was the first First Nations hockey player named to Canada's National Women's Team. She earned a silver medal at the 2018 Winter Olympics.

ALISSA PILI (2001–): Alissa Pili is a Samoan and Iñupiaq basketball player. She was the eighth player drafted in the 2024 WNBA draft. She was drafted by the Minnesota Lynx, and she has also played for the Los Angeles Sparks.

MARGARET NEWAGO PASCALE (1921–2002): Margaret was an Ojibwe woman from Wisconsin. She served in World War II, earned her GED when she was 50, and testified before Congress to stop the removal of the Red Cliff Ojibwe from their homelands in the 1960s. She was also my grandma.

GLOSSARY

ACTIVIST: Someone who works toward change

ADVOCATE: Someone who supports a cause or a group

ARTIFACT: An item made by human beings, usually a long time ago

BUREAU OF INDIAN AFFAIRS: Previously known as the Office of Indian Affairs, it is an agency of the U.S. government that works with Native nations and Native people

COMBAT MISSION: A mission to capture or defend something

DEROGATORY: A negative opinion about something or someone

DISCRIMINATION: Treating someone unfairly or differently because of who they are

ENTREPRENEUR: Someone who starts their own business

FEDERAL INDIAN BOARDING SCHOOL: One of many schools set up by the U.S. government to forcibly assimilate Native children into white American culture

FEDERAL INDIAN POLICY: The rules that Native nations and the U.S. government use to interact with each other based on a government-to-government relationship.

INDIAN AGENTS: Historically, Indian agents interacted with Native nations on behalf of the U.S. government

INDIAN RELOCATION ACT: A law that pushed Native people to move away from their reservations and into larger cities

INDIGENOUS: Belonging to or being the original people of a place

MIDWIFE: A person who is trained to help women during childbirth

NATIVE: The first people who lived (and continue to live) in what is now the United States. They may also be called "American Indian," "Native American," or "Indigenous."

POWWOW: An Indigenous event with dancing, songs, and ceremonies

PRINCIPAL CHIEF: The title given to the leader of the Cherokee Nation

REGALIA: Certain clothes that are worn for special occasions

RESERVATION: Land set aside and held in trust for Native nations in the United States

RESERVE: Land set aside and held in trust for Indigenous (First Nations) peoples in Canada

SOVEREIGNTY: The freedom that a state or nation has to control itself

STEREOTYPE: An overly simple view of someone based on a category or group they are put into

SUFFRAGIST: Someone who believes that everyone—including women—should have the right to vote

TERRITORY: The land and waters that belong to a country

TEST PILOT: A pilot who puts new aircraft through tests to make sure they're safe and will work properly

TREATY: An agreement between two or more nations

TREATY RIGHTS: Rights that have been reserved for Native nations through treaties

RESOURCES

"A Native Story," *Honest History*, Issue #15.

Anton Treuer, *Everything You Wanted to Know About Indians But Were Afraid to Ask: Young Readers Edition* (Levine Querido).

Cynthia O'Brien, *Encyclopedia of American Indian History and Culture* (National Geographic Kids).

Do All Indians Live in Tipis? Questions and Answers from the National Museum of the American Indian (Smithsonian Books).

David Grann, *Killers of the Flower Moon: Adapted for Young Readers* (Crown Books for Young Readers).

David A. Robertson, *Sugar Falls: A Residential School Story* (HighWater Press).

Michelle Cyca, "9 Facts About Native American Tribes," History.com website, history.com/articles/native-american-tribes-facts.

"Native Americans," National Geographic for Kids website, kids.nationalgeographic.com/history/topic/native-americans.

"Native Knowledge 360°," National Museum of the American Indian website, americanindian.si.edu/nk360.

Roxanne Dunbar-Ortiz, adapted by Jean Mendoza and Debbie Reese, *An Indigenous Peoples' History of the United States for Young People* (Beacon Press).

NATIVE NATIONS REPRESENTED

ANISHINAABE

Autumn Peltier

APSÁALOOKE (CROW)

Susie Walking Bear Yellowtail

BIG RIVER FIRST NATION

Sylvia McAdam Saysewahum

BLACKFEET

Elouise Cobell

Lily Gladstone [also Nez Perce]

Minnie Spotted Wolf

CHEROKEE

Wilma Mankiller

Mary Golda Ross

CHEYENNE

Suzan Shown Harjo

CITIZEN POTAWATOMI

Mary Killman

Robin Wall Kimmerer

COMANCHE

Janee' Kassanavoid

CONFEDERATED SALISH AND KOOTENAI TRIBES

Jaune Quick-to-See Smith

COTE FIRST NATION

Brigette Lacquette

DAKOTA

LaDonna Brave Bull Allard
[also Lakota]

DINÉ (NAVAJO)

Lori Arviso Alvord

Ryneldi Becenti

Jordan Marie Brings Three White Horses Daniel [also Lakota]

Madison Hammond
[also San Felipe Pueblo]

Annie Dodge Wauneka

FORT PECK ASSINIBOINE AND SIOUX TRIBES

Bonnie Red Elk

Minnie Two Shoes

HOPI

Lori Piestewa

IÑUPIAQ

Ada Blackjack

Alissa Pili [also Samoan]

Alberta Schenck

KAHKEWISTAHAW FIRST NATION

Nina Wilson

LAGUNA PUEBLO

Deb Haaland

LAKOTA

LaDonna Brave Bull Allard [also Dakota]

Jordan Marie Brings Three White Horses Daniel [also Diné]

Ola Mildred Rexroat (Oglala)

MENOMINEE

Ada Deer

MÉTIS

Jocelyne Larocque

MI'KMAW

Patti Catalano

MOHAWK

Katsi Cook

MUSCOGEE (CREEK)

Suzan Shown Harjo [also Cheyenne]

NEZ PERCE

Lily Gladstone [also Blackfeet]

NORTHERN CHEYENNE

Buffalo Calf Road Woman

OJIBWE

Ignatia Broker (White Earth)

Peggy Flanagan (White Earth)

Maude Kegg (Mille Lacs)

Margaret Newago Pascale (Red Cliff)

Olivia Poole

Jane Johnston Schoolcraft

OJIBWE OF THE WAHNAPITAE FIRST NATION

Abby Roque

OMAHA

Susan La Flesche Picotte

ONEIDA

Laura Cornelius Kellogg

OSAGE

Maria Tallchief

PASQUA FIRST NATION

Jessica Gordon

SAC AND FOX

Grace Thorpe

SAN FELIPE PUEBLO

Madison Hammond
[also Navajo/Diné]

SEMINOLE

Betty Mae Tiger Jumper

SENECA

Bertha Parker

TLINGIT

Elizabeth Peratrovich

TLINGIT AND HAIDA

Michaela Goade

TOHONO O'ODHAM

Ofelia Zepeda

TULALIP

Janet McCloud

TURTLE MOUNTAIN BAND OF CHIPPEWA INDIANS

Marie Louise Bottineau Baldwin

Louise Erdrich

WAILACKI OF THE ROUND VALLEY INDIAN TRIBES

Nicole Aunapu Mann

WAMPANOAG

Elizabeth James-Perry

WINNEBAGO (HO-CHUNK)

Angel De Cora

Lorelei DeCora Means

WYANDOT

Eliza "Lyda" Conley

YANKTON DAKOTA

Maria Pearson

Faith Spotted Eagle

Mary Sully

Zitkala-Ša

ACKNOWLEDGMENTS

This book, as with all the books I write, would not be possible without the love and support of my family. My parents always gave me the space to follow my dreams, and their continuous faith in me has carried me to where I am today. I probably don't say "thank you" as often as I should, so hopefully this makes up for it. I'm grateful for the friends, colleagues, and extended family who always cheer me on and share my work. And, last but not least, there are Jake, Leo, and Max—this is, as always, for you.

ABOUT THE AUTHOR

Dr. Katrina Phillips is from the Red Cliff Band of Lake Superior Ojibwe, and she was born and raised in northern Wisconsin, along the south shore of Lake Superior. She grew up reading just about every book she could find, so it makes sense that she earned a BA and a PhD in history from the University of Minnesota. She's a history professor at Macalester College and has written numerous children's books, including *Indigenous Peoples' Day* and *I Am on Indigenous Land*. She lives in the Twin Cities with her husband, their two boys, and their two dogs. Her favorite food is chocolate.

ABOUT THE ILLUSTRATOR

TΔI is a visual artivist and communicator born in Belém (PA), with a bachelor's degree in fashion and a master's degree in communication and semiotics from PUC-SP.

She creates encantados and visagentos universes through illustrations and comic books, based on her urban Amazonian roots and the recovery of her ancestral culture, using colors as her main allies to express her perception of the world and her spirituality.

She has worked for companies such as Grendha, Microsoft, and Companhia das Letras. She is also an award-winning author as Best Screenwriter in the Mapinguari Comics Award and has three HQMIX Trophies for the comic book "Onde Habita o Medo" (Where Fear Lives) (2024), in addition to being one of the organizers of the Circuito Amazônico de Quadrinhos.

EXPLORE THE SERIES AND MEET EVEN MORE HEROES!

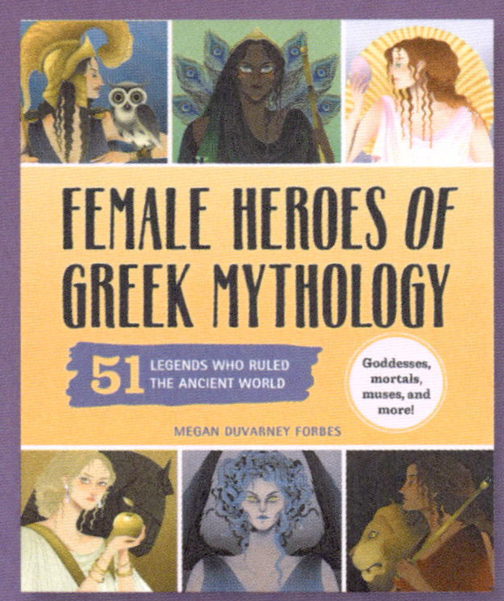

WHOSE STORY WILL INSPIRE YOU?